PRACTICE
MAKES
PERFECT™

Chemistry

PRACTICE
MAKES
PERFECT™

Chemistry

Heather R. Hattori and Marian L. DeWane

Mc
Graw
Hill

New York   Chicago   San Francisco   Lisbon   London   Madrid   Mexico City
Milan   New Delhi   San Juan   Seoul   Singapore   Sydney   Toronto

1 2 3 4 5 6 7 8 9 10 11 12 13 14 15 16   QDB/QDB   1 9 8 7 6 5 4 3 2 1

ISBN   978-0-07-174549-9
MHID   0-07-174549-1

e-ISBN   978-0-07-174695-3
e-MHID   0-07-174695-1

Library of Congress Control Number 2010941609

Interior design by Village Bookworks, Inc.
Interior illustrations by Glyph International

McGraw-Hill books are available at special quantity discounts to use as premiums and
sales promotions or for use in corporate training programs. To contact a representative,
please e-mail us at bulksales@mcgraw-hill.com.

This book is printed on acid-free paper.

Contents

5 Naming compounds and writing formulas 57

6 Chemical reactions 73

7 Mass and mole relationships 91

Preface

Chemistry is a science where the concrete, macroscopic world we see results from a microscopic world that continues to be explored and investigated. These explorations and investigations help scientists to develop models that can and do change as technology allows the scientists to improve their observations and increase their data-collecting abilities.

A model can be explained most simply as a representation or explanation of an object or process that an investigator is familiar with and is trying to communicate to another investigator, the general public, or a novice learner. In chemistry we use physical, mathematical, and conceptual models. Physical models help one to visualize how an object or process works. They often contain adjustable parts and are built to scale, like a model airplane or a watershed model, or a model of a chemical molecule. Mathematical models explain phenomena using equations to fit existing data and predict what occurs when a change is made in a system. An example of this might be expressing a relationship and predicting the change in the volume of a gas when the temperature is increased (as we will see in Chapter 8). Conceptual models describe ideas or processes in terms of concrete objects, sometimes expressing them as an analogy. Saying that the cell nucleus is the city hall of the cell and that the mitochondria are the power plants would be an example of a conceptual model. A chemistry example is the analogy of electron configurations in atoms to addresses on a street, as seen in Chapter 4.

Models, symbols, words, and mathematics are the tools of chemistry. Whether we are talking about a model of an atom as in Chapter 3, the abbreviation H (the symbol for hydrogen), or α, the Greek letter alpha (a symbolic representation of a helium atom with nuclear notation of $_2^4He$), chemistry may feel like a whole new language. Familiar words like *nucleus*, *periodic*, and *mole* may take on new meaning after studying chemistry. You may even be introduced to a few new words and phrases, like *hydroxide*, *molality*, and *colligative properties*. In terms of mathematics, a basic knowledge of arithmetic and algebra as well as access to a basic scientific calculator will be helpful for many sections in this text.

The goal of this book is to help you achieve an understanding of the models, symbols, and essential concepts of chemistry. You will establish a solid foundation through the use of critical vocabulary. Building this foundation on fundamental chemical concepts will help you avert misconceptions. Numerous sample problems and extensive exercises will test your expanding knowledge base and allow you to put into practice what you've learned.

Objective questions about concepts and problem-solving skills presented test your expanding knowledge base and check for understanding each step along the way. We hope that by focusing special attention on areas that have traditionally given learners difficulty, we will help you avoid frustration.

Chemistry—a subject studied by many and feared by some—opens the door to understanding the everyday world. By selecting this book you are challenging the perception that chemistry is both difficult and unattainable. We hope you will acquire an enduring understanding of the fundamental chemical concepts presented, if you use just a few chapters or the entire book. Whether you are currently a student or are a lifelong learner, this book offers succinct explanations of basic chemical concepts, worked examples of commonly encountered problems, and opportunities for you to practice the skills presented. The key to success in chemistry is the same as in any other academic endeavor—practice. Each section provides multiple opportunities to practice the same type of problem, so if you master a skill after a couple problems, feel free to go on to the next section.

May the practice provided here be the key to your success! Good luck on your journey!

Acknowledgments

Ms. Hattori would like to express her gratitude to Drs. John T. Moore and Richard H. Langley. Without their numerous books, tireless dedication to writing, and recommendation to Grace, this opportunity among others would have never come her way. Ms. Hattori would also like to thank her patient writing partner, Marian, for putting up with her busy nature.

Ms. DeWane would like to express her gratitude to her family for being patient, to Dr. John T. Moore and Dr. Richard H. Langley for support, to Dr. George E. Miller and Dr. Thomas J. Greenbowe for reviewing chapters, to Ms. Grace Freedson for this opportunity, and most of all to Heather for working on this project with her. This project has enabled them to recognize each other's strengths and weaknesses, and in the process develop a closer friendship.

**PRACTICE
MAKES
PERFECT**™

Chemistry

Matter

Classification, properties, and changes

Classification of matter

All matter can be classified as a substance or mixture depending on its composition. The word *substance* refers to elements or compounds with an exact chemical composition. *Elements* are composed of only one type of atom, such as hydrogen, H_2; *compounds* are composed of two or more types of atoms maintaining an exact ratio, such as water, H_2O.

In contrast, *mixtures*, such as lemonade, do not have such an exact composition, though overall they may have approximately fixed ratios of components. Mixtures can be identified as homogeneous or heterogeneous. *Homogeneous mixtures*, like clear lemonade, are also called *solutions*, since all the component parts are uniformly distributed and appear as one thing, which may have a certain concentration, but can be made to have almost any composition. Another example is air. The amount of different gases in air varies by place, time of day, and weather. The individual components in the mixtures retain their identity, such as the elements nitrogen (N_2) and oxygen (O_2) and the compound carbon dioxide (CO_2). The air also can be classified as heterogeneous.

Heterogeneous mixtures usually have visibly different components, which may be seen with the aid of instruments rather than the naked eye. This might be when you can see particulate matter such as black soot coming out the tailpipe of a truck into the air, or when using a microscope you can see different types of blood cells unevenly distributed. Other examples of heterogeneous mixtures would be Jell-O with fruit in it that can be seen, and uncut fruitcake that contains both external (seen) and internal (unseen) variations. Figure 1.1 shows how matter can be classified by its components.

Elements are substances that contain only one type of atom. *Atoms* cannot be separated into smaller units by normal means, but they can be broken down by nuclear reactions. (This will be discussed in Chapter 3.) Compounds, which have formulas to represent them, can, through chemical reactions, be broken into the atoms of elements composing them.

Mixtures are different, since they are not held together through the bonding of atoms; physical methods like filtering, sifting, and heating can recover the individual parts of the mixture. Marshmallows can be removed from hot cocoa. A saltwater solution can be separated into pure water and salt using distillation.

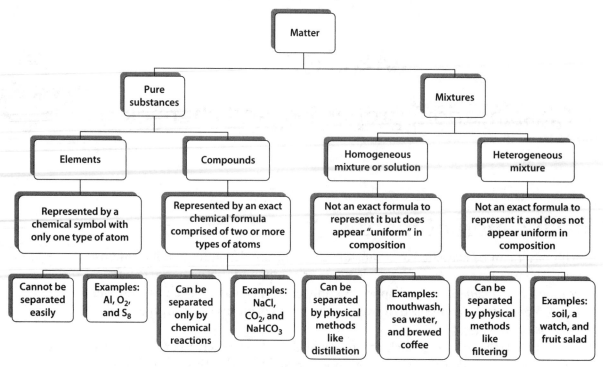

Figure 1.1

A question you can ask to help determine what type of matter you have might be, "Is there a way to get back the original components?" Can iron filings be separated from sand using a magnet? Yes—you can see the black iron filings in the light-colored sand—so that is a heterogeneous mixture.

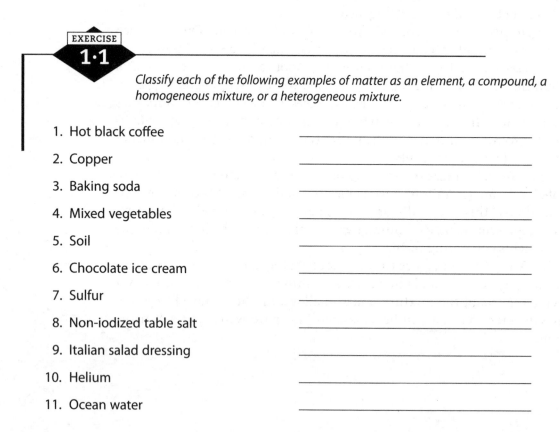

EXERCISE

1·1

Classify each of the following examples of matter as an element, a compound, a homogeneous mixture, or a heterogeneous mixture.

1. Hot black coffee _____

2. Copper _____

3. Baking soda _____

4. Mixed vegetables _____

5. Soil _____

6. Chocolate ice cream _____

7. Sulfur _____

8. Non-iodized table salt _____

9. Italian salad dressing _____

10. Helium _____

11. Ocean water _____

12. Dry ice _____

13. Aluminum foil _____

14. A cheeseburger _____

15. Vitamin C _____

Properties of matter

Substances can be distinguished by their properties. These properties can be either physical or chemical. *Physical properties* can be observed or measured without changing the formula of the substance. *Chemical properties* are observed when a substance changes or does not change in a chemical reaction. Physical properties include melting point, boiling point, color, electrical conductivity, malleability, ductility, luster, density, and phase (solid, liquid, gas, or plasma—although we will not be studying plasmas in this book) at a set temperature and pressure. *Malleability* is how easily a metal can be molded into shapes, like a flat sheet, and ductility is its ability to be drawn into a wire. For example, lead is very soft and malleable and copper is very ductile.

Some physical properties depend on how much matter is present. These are called *extensive* properties; examples include mass and volume. If more matter is present, the mass will be greater and the space occupied will be greater. Properties that do not depend on the amount of matter present are called *intensive*. Temperature and density are examples of intensive properties. (Density will be discussed in a later section.)

Chemical properties are indications of either reactivity or non-reactivity with another substance. Iron can oxidize (rust) in air, indicating a chemical change. If it rusts, it changes from Fe to Fe_2O_3. Methane (CH_4) can burn with the oxygen gas in the air with a flame to change to into carbon dioxide and water. A substance with acidic properties can react with a base, chemically changing to form a salt and water. In each case of chemical change, the linking of the atoms changes (e.g., when CH_4 becomes CO_2 the carbon is now linked or bonded differently than before the change).

EXERCISE

1·2

Identify each of the following properties as being either physical or chemical.

1. Green color _____

2. Mass _____

3. Flammability _____

4. Freezing point _____

5. Reactivity with acid to form hydrogen _____

6. Boiling point at 90°C _____

7. Malleability _____

8. Resistance to corrosion _____

9. Conductivity of electricity _____

10. Dissolution in water _____

Identify each of the following properties as being either intensive or extensive.

11. Color   _____

12. Length   _____

13. Melting point   _____

14. Height   _____

15. Solubility in water at 20°C   _____

16. Mass   _____

17. Ductility   _____

18. Boiling point   _____

19. Density   _____

20. Conductivity   _____

Changes in matter

Physical change results when the amount or phase of a substance is changed but it is still the same substance. For instance, cutting a piece of copper in half does not change the copper to silver—there are just two pieces of copper. The physical form has changed but it is still the same substance. Another example is freezing water: ice is still H_2O, but instead of it being a liquid it is a solid.

In contrast, a chemical change changes the formula of the substance, since it has undergone a chemical reaction with another substance (see Figure 1.2). When iron (Fe) reacts with the oxygen (O_2) in the air to make iron(III) oxide (Fe_2O_3)—or, as it is more commonly known, rust—this is an example of a chemical change. Words that commonly indicate a chemical change include *flammability*, *corrosiveness*, *reactivity*, and *oxidation*. Household examples include iron rusting, milk souring, grass decomposing, and an egg frying. In each case, something with a new chemical composition is formed.

Physical properties of substances describe unchanging composition characteristics, while chemical properties describe chemical behaviors with other substances that result in composition (atom-linking arrangement) changes.

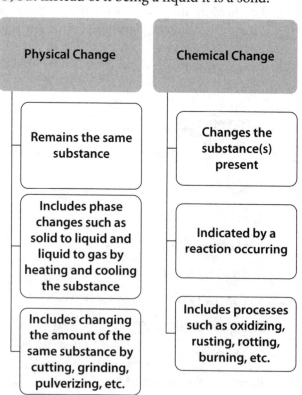

Figure 1.2

EXERCISE 1·3

Indicate which of the changes below are chemical. Check that the ones you don't mark are physical changes.

1. Wood rots _____
2. Ice melts _____
3. A cake bakes _____
4. Paper is cut _____
5. A plant dies _____
6. Silver is made into a thin wire _____
7. A car is dented _____
8. Water is heated and turned into steam _____
9. Alcohol evaporates _____
10. A battery charges _____
11. A piece of cake is split in two _____
12. A piece of metal rusts _____
13. Green leaves turn orange in fall _____
14. A letter is opened _____
15. Paint dries _____

Density

Another physical property is density. *Density* is the ratio of the amount of matter present (mass) to the amount of space that matter occupies (volume). In other words, density is the ratio of mass to volume of a substance. For any substance (elements and compounds), the ratio remains constant at a given set of conditions.

Standard densities are reported at 1 atmosphere of pressure and a temperature of 25°C. The density of a substance can be used as an identifying property. Someone selling 24-karat (pure) gold could be easily checked, since the density of 24-karat gold is 19.3 g/cm³, the density of 22-karat gold is 17.7 g/cm³, and the density of 18-karat gold only 15.5 g/cm³ (see Table 1.1).

Table 1.1 Density of Substances at 20°C

Substance	Density in g/cm³	Substance	Density in g/mL
Gold	19.3	Acetone	0.79
Iron	7.9	Ethanol	0.772
Mercury	13.6	Gasoline	0.70
Silver	10.5	Hexane	0.658
Sodium chloride	2.2	Water	0.998
Zinc	7.14		

Identifying an unknown metal can be easily accomplished using the property of density. Measuring a mass of 62.5 g and a volume of 6.00 cm^3 for a metal gives a ratio of 10.4 to 1. The metal is most likely silver.

Answer the following questions rounding the answer to three total digits. A discussion about proper rounding will be presented in Chapter 2.

1. A gold ring was purchased from a street vendor for a ridiculously low price. The buyer has brought the ring to you to confirm its metal content. You have found the mass of the ring to be 23.46 g and its volume to be 2.25 cm^3. What do you tell the buyer?

2. In order to make coins that have less mass but will still fit into vending machines, a country is looking at different metals to substitute for the ones that they presently use. Unfortunately, a technician forgot to include the identities of the metals with the test results. What metals were tested if the following table represents the results?

SAMPLE	MASS	VOLUME	IDENTITY
Metal 1	55.33 g	7.75 cm^3	_____
Metal 2	61.5 g	4.52 cm^3	_____
Metal 3	19.4 g	2.45 cm^3	_____

3. Determine the volume that 45.8 g of carbon tetrachloride will occupy if it has a density of 1.60 g/mL.

4. Determine the mass of zinc that will occupy 18.6 cm^3 if it has a density of 7.14 g/cm^3.

5. What is the density of lead if a piece of lead 1.00 cm by 20.0 cm by 30.0 cm has a mass of 6,800 g?

6. A sheet of aluminum has a mass of 27.0 g and measurements of 10.0 cm by 1.00 cm by 1.00 cm. Calculate the density of aluminum.

7. What is the density of a saltwater solution that has a mass of 17.84 g and a volume of 15.00 mL?

8. A piece of wood has a mass of 27.0 kg and a volume of 15.4 dm³. What is its density, and will it sink or float in water?

9. At 20°C, what mass of ethanol will occupy 250 mL?

10. Platinum has a density of 21.410 g/cm³. What volume of platinum has a mass of 50.0 g?

Graphical analysis of density

When comparing measured values for different-sized samples of a material, the plot of volume versus mass will result in a straight line. The slope of this line represents the density. Given the data in Table 1.2, a graph such as the one in Figure 1.3 can be made. By making a best-fit line through the points, the ratio of 1.0 to 1.0 is obtained. This means that no matter how the mass changes, the volume will change by the same ratio. If the mass is halved, the volume will also halve. If the mass is tripled, the volume will triple. This relationship is called a *direct relationship*, and since the slope always has the same value, this confirms that density is an intensive property.

Table 1.2 Density of Water at 25°C

Mass (in g)	Volume (in mL)
1.0	1.0
3.5	3.5
5.0	5.0
8.0	8.0
12.0	12.0
18.0	18.0
22.0	22.0
30.0	30.0
43.0	43.0

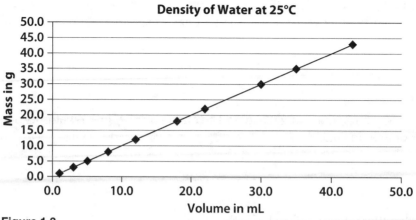

Figure 1.3

Use the following graph and Table 1.1 on page 5 to answer questions 1 and 2.

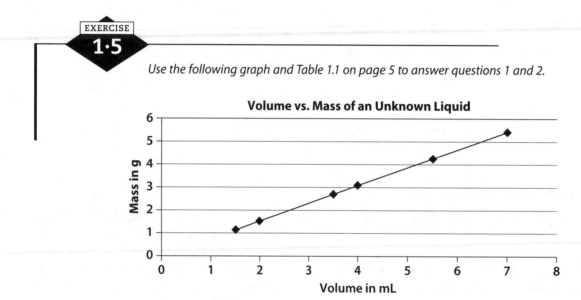

1. The density of the unknown liquid is _____.

2. The identity of the unknown liquid is _____.

Use the information in the following table to answer questions 3 through 5.

Mass in g	Volume in mL
1.10	2.42
3.60	7.92
4.10	9.02
5.30	11.7
5.70	12.6

3. Using the data from the table, draw a graph of the volume versus the mass. Draw a best-fit line through the data and determine the slope of the line.

4. What is the density of the unknown object? _____

5. If it does not dissolve, will this substance sink beneath or float on the liquid in problems 1 and 2 of this exercise? _____

EXERCISE
1·6

Classify each of the following substances by placing a check mark in the appropriate column.

SUBSTANCE	ELEMENT	COMPOUND	HOMOGENOUS MIXTURE	HETEROGENEOUS MIXTURE
1. Grape jelly	_____	_____	_____	_____
2. Neon gas	_____	_____	_____	_____
3. Trail mix	_____	_____	_____	_____
4. Water	_____	_____	_____	_____
5. Beef stew	_____	_____	_____	_____

EXERCISE
1·7

Classify each of the following properties by placing check marks in the appropriate columns.

PROPERTY	PHYSICAL	CHEMICAL	INTENSIVE	EXTENSIVE
1. Boiling point	_____	_____	_____	_____
2. Height	_____	_____	_____	_____
3. Reactivity with water	_____	_____	_____	_____
4. Blue color	_____	_____	_____	_____

5. Toxicity ——————— ——————— ——————— ———————

6. Density ——————— ——————— ——————— ———————

Indicate whether the following changes are physical, chemical, or both by placing a check mark in the appropriate column.

CHANGE	PHYSICAL	CHEMICAL	BOTH
1. An incandescent bulb burns out	———————	———————	———————
2. A spoon is bent	———————	———————	———————
3. Bread molds	———————	———————	———————
4. Soda goes flat	———————	———————	———————
5. Sweat evaporates	———————	———————	———————
6. A lightbulb lights up	———————	———————	———————
7. Copper is electroplated	———————	———————	———————
8. Food is digested	———————	———————	———————
9. An egg is hard-boiled	———————	———————	———————
10. A propane barbecue is ignited	———————	———————	———————

Calculate the missing numeric value(s), rounding the answer to two total digits, and if not given, determine the identity of the unknown substance. All substances are at 20°C.

SUBSTANCE	MASS	VOLUME	DENSITY	IDENTITY
1	———————	$1.1\ cm^3$	$19.3\ g/cm^3$	———————
2	9.95 g	12.6 mL	———————	———————
3	1.056 g	———————	———————	sodium chloride
4	———————	$4.39\ cm^3$	———————	iron
5	25 g	———————	0.658 g/mL	———————

Measurement, mathematical notations, and conversions

The metric system

The *International System of Units* is the system of science. This system uses the metric system. There are standard units you will need to practice working with in order to be comfortable: these include units for *mass* (grams), *length* (meters), and *volume* (liters). Some of the common prefixes in chemistry that may appear in front of the standard unit name include *deci-* (0.1), *centi-* (0.01), and *milli-* (0.001). Science most frequently uses *scientific notation* for expressing numerical values. Often a chemist will need to change between units, so understanding the size of a unit and its representation in scientific notation is important (see Table 2.1).

Table 2.1 Metric Prefixes

Prefix and symbol	Common word	Numeric notation	Scientific notation
tera-, T	trillion	1,000,000,000,000	1×10^{12}
giga-, G	billion	1,000,000,000	1×10^{9}
mega-, M	million	1,000,000	1×10^{6}
kilo-, k	thousand	1,000	1×10^{3}
hecto-, h	hundred	100	1×10^{2}
deca-, da	ten	10	1×10^{1}
deci-, d	tenth	0.1	1×10^{-1}
centi-, c	hundredth	0.01	1×10^{-2}
milli-, m	thousandth	0.001	1×10^{-3}
micro-, μ	millionth	0.000001	1×10^{-6}
nano-, n	billionth	0.000000001	1×10^{-9}
pico-, p	trillionth	0.000000000001	1×10^{-12}

Knowing the size of a unit will be important in dimensional analysis, which involves changing from one unit to another. Knowing there are 100 centimeters in 1 meter gives two possible ratios to use:

$$\frac{1 \text{ m}}{100 \text{ cm}} \text{ and } \frac{100 \text{ cm}}{1 \text{ m}}$$

How are measurements written? Measured values should always include units, and often scientific notation will be used. This notation will include only place values that were measured. How to make actual measurements will be covered in a later section, as will practicing conversions.

Any numeral 1 to 9 in a measurement is a measured value; the question is the 0—was it measured or is it a placeholder? Some statements of measurement, such as 120 g, are unclear, since the 0 is just a placeholder if only the hundreds and tens values were measured. If the placeholder 0 were left off, the measurement would be 12 and not 120 g. Just looking at the number, one does not know if the 0 was actually measured. This is where scientific notation is advantageous; this 0 would not be written in scientific notation if it is only a placeholder. We will address this concept in more detail in the section on significant figures.

To write in scientific notation, only one digit can be placed in front of the decimal point. Other measured digits are behind the decimal point. A measurement of 120 g would then be 1.2×10^2 g—or 1.20×10^2 g if the 0 were indeed part of the measurement. This way of expressing values is very clear as to the accuracy of the measurement. To determine the nonscientific notation measurement of 291 g, the number 2.91 is multiplied by 100, or 10^2. This then would have been written in scientific notation as 2.91×10^2 g. A measurement of 1.35×10^3 g could be 1,350 g, but it could also be 1,352 g or 1,348 g—we don't know for sure. On the other hand, 1.350×10^3 g is *definitely* 1,350 g. Small values are treated the same way, but with negative exponents: 0.0055 g is 5.5×10^{-3} g.

Generally, the exponents of 1 (10^1 and 10^{-1}) are not used, though this can lead to some uncertainty. Is the value 10 g exactly 10 g or is it only approximately 10 g? Using 1.0×10^1 would be more certain but is not common practice. Another way to express that value is 10. g (notice the decimal point after the 0).

EXERCISE
2·1

Express the following measured values in scientific notation.

1. 750 g (measured to the tens place) _____

2. 94,632 mL _____

3. 0.010 kg (measured to the thousandths place) _____

4. 0.0058 L _____

5. 200,000 mg (measured to the thousands place) _____

6. 802.0 g _____

7. 5,050.0 mL _____

8. 220. mL _____

9. 0.00101 g _____

10. 0.002 g _____

Express the following values as numbers.

11. 5.1×10^{-4} cm _____

12. 2.8×10^3 g _____

13. 5.2101×10^2 mL   _____

14. 6.33×10^{-5} km   _____

15. 4.60×10^3 g   _____

16. 4×10^{-4} cm^3 _____

17. 1.600×10^2 g   _____

18. 2.834×10^6 g   _____

19. 3.240×10^{-4} mL   _____

20. 2.705×10^{-1} g   _____

Accuracy in measurements

When a measurement is going to be made, it is important to consider the device being used. No device is perfect; therefore, one should consider the accuracy of the devices being considered. The one that can give a measurement closest to the true value is the best. When reading a device such as a beaker or graduated cylinder, look at the marks present. (See Figures 2.1, 2.2, 2.3, and 2.4 for examples of these devices.) A measurement reads by place value the units marked, and then an estimate is made for the next smaller place value. The unit markings you can use are in metric units of hundredths, tenths, ones, tens, hundreds, and so on.

Figure 2.1

If the markings are at 10 mL, 20 mL, and 30 mL, and so on, the place value you can read is the tens. The next smaller place value is the ones, so a measurement made can be recorded only to the ones place. The measurement in Figure 2.1 would be 26 mL, not 26.0 mL.

Figure 2.2

Water and aqueous solutions exhibit a downward curvature in the liquid surface, called a _meniscus_, when in a glass container. If the bottom of the meniscus is right on the 20 mL marking, as in Figure 2.2, then a decimal is put after the 0 (20. mL) or the number is written in scientific notation (2.0×10^1 mL). Why is this important? It is difficult otherwise to determine from the written record of a measurement whether the value represented by a 0 was actually measured.

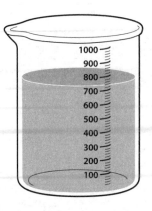

Figure 2.3

What if the beaker is marked at 100 mL, 200 mL, and so on, as in Figure 2.3? The next place value would be the tens. A measurement of 740 mL would be possible. Here the 0 is a placeholder only and does not represent a value that was measured. There would not be a decimal point after the 0, and if written in scientific notation, the number would be 7.4×10^2 mL.

EXERCISE
2·2

Using the figure provided, record the measurement at each marked location.

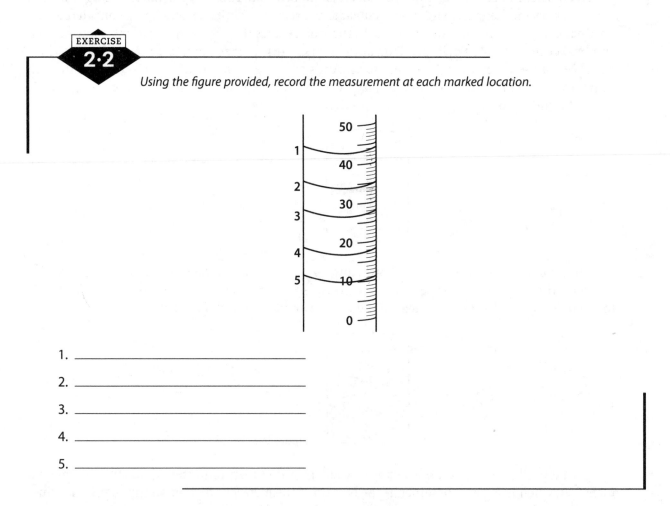

1. _____

2. _____

3. _____

4. _____

5. _____

Using the figures below (note the different scales), record the volume of each substance being measured. The unit used on each device is milliliters.

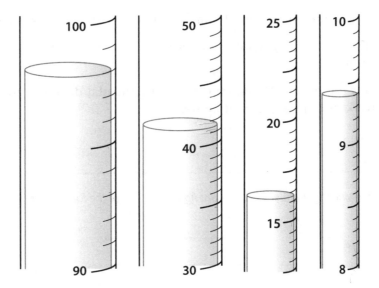

1. _____

2. _____

3. _____

4. _____

Significant figures

The digits measured in a measurement and expressed as its value are called significant figures ("sig figs"). One of the ways scientists communicate their results to other scientists is by using significant figures. For instance, if you polled 10 people and 9 liked pepperoni on their pizza, you could say 90% of people prefer pepperoni. What if you asked 100 people, 1,000 people, or 10,000 people? Does 90% really tell you anything unless you know about sample size? Significant figures would distinguish them as 90.%, 90.0%, 90.00%, and 90.000%. Significant figures also affect the way mathematical operations are done. The number of significant figures reported is important when doing mathematical operations. Before doing mathematical operations, you must understand how many digits in each value are actually significant. Counting sig figs requires practice and knowledge of measurements. Here are some rules to help:

- The numerals 1 through 9 are *always* significant.

    1,247 g has four sig figs.

- Zeros that begin numbers are *never* significant. They are only placeholders.

    0.021 g has two sig figs.

- Zeros that are between the numerals 1 through 9 are *always* significant.

    102 g has three sig figs.

◆ Zeros that trail a number may or may not have been measured—it depends on the presence of a decimal point! If a decimal point *is present*, the trailing 0 was measured.

370 g has two sig figs. No decimal point is present, so the 0 is a placeholder. A better way to display this value would be 3.7×10^2 g.

370. g has three sig figs. The decimal point indicates that the 0 was measured.

0.0250 g has three sig figs. The leading 0s are placeholders, but the trailing 0 was measured.

So why is this important? When reporting experimental data, scientists communicate the details of their work through significant figures.

EXERCISE 2·4

Determine the number of significant figures in each of the following numbers.

1. 110 m _____
2. 633 g _____
3. 900 mL _____
4. 0.250 g _____
5. 8.08 m _____
6. 0.0007446 km _____
7. 5,000,000 g _____
8. 40. L _____
9. 0.007310 kg _____
10. 0.227568 Mm _____
11. 0.157 kg _____
12. 2,500 m _____
13. 0.0250 cm³ _____
14. 2.680 g _____
15. 44.07 cm _____
16. 50.00 g _____
17. 21 mL _____
18. 8.28 km _____
19. 6.0001 g _____
20. 0.01 g _____

Calculations with significant figures

When making calculations with significant figures, there are additional rules to follow. Two rules apply to the basic mathematical operations of addition, subtraction, multiplication, and division.

- When adding or subtracting two or more measurements, round the answer to the least-accurate decimal place measured. It is also vital that the values be expressed in the same units.

    35.74 mL − 2.4 mL = 33.3 mL

    When this difference is set up as

    35.74 mL
    −2.4 mL

    you can see that the last digit in 35.74 has no digit under it. Since one number was measured to the hundredths place and the other to the tenths place, the least-accurate decimal place is the tenths.

> If the measurements being subtracted or added are given in scientific notation, it is better to first convert the values to the same scientific expression. For example, 13.578×10^2 g − 6.2355×10^{-1} g = 13.572 g can be rewritten as 13.578×10^2 g − 0.0062355×10^2 g to make the placement of the last significant figure more apparent.

- When multiplying or dividing measurements, count the number of sig figs in the numbers and round the answer to the smallest number of sig figs.

    2.50 cm × 1.2 cm = 3.0 cm², not 3.00 cm², since 2.50 cm has three significant figures and 1.2 cm has two significant figures.

- Exact numbers used in a conversion *do not* count in sig figs (more on this in a couple sections).

    1 kg = 1,000 g

- When a number needs to be rounded, look at only the first digit past the last significant figure. If it is a 5 or higher, round up the last significant figure; if it is a 4 or lower, leave the last significant figure as it is written.

    27.56 g rounded to three significant figures is 27.6 g; 27.46 g rounded to two significant figures is 27 g.

> Sometimes a combination of operations can occur. In that case, the subtraction and addition are completed and rounded first before the multiplication and division are done. An example of this is solving for density using the water-displacement method.

Density is the ratio of the mass to the volume of an object. Assume water is placed in a 100. mL graduated cylinder with a measurement of 62.7 mL before a solid object is submerged in the water. The final volume of the water and the object is 79.2 mL. The object has a mass of 12.875 g. What is the density of the object? First, we must do the subtraction. Both values are measured to the tenths place, so the final answer is rounded to the tenths place: 79.2 mL − 62.7 mL = 16.5 mL.

Next, the division step can be done. A five-digit mass is being divided by a three-digit volume, so the answer must be rounded to three sig figs.

$$\frac{12.875\,\text{g}}{16.5\,\text{mL}} = 0.780\,\text{g/mL}$$

If the problem involves multiple operations but is all multiplication and division, round only once at the end instead of after each operation! When rounding numbers, look *only* at the first digit after the last significant figure. 32.45 g rounded to two digits is 32 g; 32.54 g rounded to two digits is 33 g.

EXERCISE

2·5

Complete the following calculations, expressing your answers with the correct number of significant figures.

1. 5.5 m + 0.781 m = _____

2. 907 mL − 65.2 mL = _____

3. 30.75 cm − 9 cm + 15.3 cm = _____

4. 1240 mg + 38.6 mg − 471.22 mg = _____

5. 9.307 m × 1.5 m = _____

6. 253.14 cm³ ÷ 7.58 cm² = _____

7. $\dfrac{0.584\,\text{kg}}{4.1\,\text{m} \times 2.36\,\text{m} \times 0.075\,\text{m}} =$ _____

8. $\dfrac{7.83\,\text{m} - 1\,\text{m}}{7.83\,\text{m}} =$ _____

9. 18.5 cm + 8 cm + 4.73 cm = _____

10. 35.0 m / 200 s = _____

11. 39.0 g ÷ 25.82 mL = _____

12. (25.43 cm − 12.0 cm) × 14.37 cm = _____

13. 3.15 dm × 4.0 dm = _____

14. 350.0 m − 200 m = _____

15. 16.53 cm − 6.3 cm = _____

16. 3.00 m × 5.2 m = _____

17. 13.563 L − 11 L = _____

18. 15.54 g + 12 g = _____

19. 0.075 g ÷ 0.003 cm³ = _____

20. 132 g + 10.00 g + 9.6 g = _____

Accuracy vs. precision

When looking at the devices in Figure 2.4, look at the measurements—if calibrated correctly, which device should give a measurement closer to the real or true value?

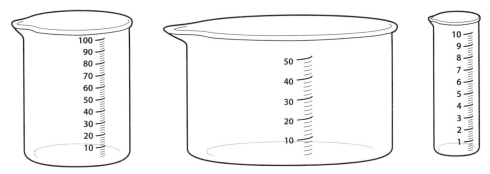

Figure 2.4

When comparing measurements, the one closest to the true value is said to be the most accurate. How does this compare to precision? Precision is how close a group of repeated measurements are to one another.

Look at the following measurements taken by different lab groups measuring the mass of the same material. The true value is 3.00 g.

	Group 1	**Group 2**	**Group 3**
Measurement 1	2.99 g	2.88 g	2.99 g
Measurement 2	2.50 g	2.87 g	2.98 g
Measurement 3	2.65 g	2.89 g	3.01 g
Average	2.71 g	2.88 g	2.99 g

Group 1's measurements lack both accuracy and precision. The measurements are not close one another, differing from the highest to lowest (called the range) by ±0.49, and are not close to the true value, with an average of 2.71 g.

Group 2's measurements have a precision range of ±0.02 (the range from the highest measurement to the lowest measurement)—the measurements are close to one another—but although more accurate than group 1, with an average of 2.88 g, they are not as accurate as group 3, with an average of 2.99 g.

Inaccuracy is often due to a device not being calibrated. If you get on a bathroom scale and it reads 112 pounds repeatedly, but your true weight is 125 pounds, the scale needs to be recalibrated. You would be getting measurements close to one another, so high precision, but not close to the true value of your weight. Group 3's measurements have a precision of ±0.03—not quite as good as group 2's measurements, but they are more accurate, since their measurements are closer to the real value.

EXERCISE
2·6

1. Two students went into the lab and measured the volume of water in the same graduated cylinder. Student 1 recorded the following measurements: 45.2 mL, 42.2 mL, and 43.3 mL. Student 2 recorded the following measurements: 43.9 mL, 43.5 mL, and 43.8 mL. The teacher had actually placed 43.7 mL of water in the graduated cylinder. Which student's measurements were more accurate? Which student's measurements were more precise?

Use the terms accurate *and* precise *to describe the shots fired at the targets in the figure provided.*

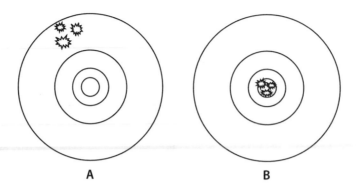

2. The shots on target A are _____ .

3. The shots on target B are _____ .

Dimensional analysis

Often in chemistry, units need to be changed to other units. This is done through a process called *dimensional analysis*. It is usually just a set of multiplication steps using what are called conversion factors. A *conversion factor* is simply the ratio of two measurements to each other. This was introduced in the section on the metric system, where the ratios $\dfrac{1\text{ m}}{100\text{ cm}}$ and $\dfrac{100\text{ cm}}{1\text{ m}}$ both state the relationship between the two units. In dimensional analysis, the conversion factor to use is the one that cancels units. For instance, the simplest conversion would be a one-step problem such as changing 5.89 mL into L.

$$58.9 \text{ mL} \times \frac{1\text{ L}}{1{,}000\text{ mL}} = 0.0589 \text{ L, also written as } 5.89 \times 10^{-2} \text{ L}$$

The two possible ratios are: $\dfrac{1\text{ L}}{1{,}000\text{ mL}}$ and $\dfrac{1{,}000\text{ mL}}{1\text{ L}}$. The ratio used has the units set up to cancel so that the correct unit remains.

A two-step problem might be changing 37.0 km/hr into m/s. This requires more steps, with each conversion done in a separate step: km to m and hr to s.

$$\frac{37.0 \text{ km}}{1\text{ hr}} \times \frac{1{,}000\text{ m}}{1\text{ km}} \times \frac{1\text{ hr}}{3{,}600\text{ s}} = 10.3 \text{ m/s, also written as } 10.3 \text{ ms}^{-1}$$

Conversion problems can range from one step to many steps. This skill is important to master!

Write in the blanks the conversion factor(s) needed to complete the following conversions.

1. 2.5 kg to g _____

2. 0.783 L to mL _____

3. 91.4 cm to m _____

4. 6.0 m/min to m/s _____

5. 0.846 m/s to km/hr _____

6. 0.75 kg to mg _____

7. 1,500 nm to km _____

8. 0.52 kg to g _____

9. 65 cm to km _____

10. 1.00 day to s _____

Using the conversion factor(s) selected above, complete the conversions using dimensional analysis, and record your answers in the blanks provided.

1. 2.5 kg to g _____

2. 0.783 L to mL _____

3. 91.4 cm to m _____

4. 6.0 m/min to m/s _____

5. 0.846 m/s to km/hr _____

6. 0.75 kg to mg _____

7. 1,500 nm to km _____

8. 0.52 kg to g _____

9. 65 cm to km _____

10. 1.00 day to s _____

Any relationship can be used as a conversion factor. In Chapter 1 density calculations were covered. Density is a ratio that can be used as a conversion factor! For example, if a substance has a density of 2.50 g/cm³ and there are 8.50 g of it, what volume would the sample occupy?

$$8.50 \ \cancel{g} \times \frac{1 \ cm^3}{2.50 \ \cancel{g}} = 3.40 \ cm^3$$

The density ratio was arranged to have units cancel, so the final answer has the units of volume, in this case, cubic centimeters.

EXERCISE

2·9

Using dimensional analysis, solve the following problems.

1. What is the mass of 4.5 cm³ of gold with a density of 19.3 g/cm³?

_____

2. What volume does a 250 g sample of mercury occupy? The density of mercury is 13.6 g/mL.

_____

3. What volume of hydrochloric acid solution with a density of 1.16 g/mL is needed to obtain a mass of 51.4 g?

_____

4. If the density of nitric acid is 1.25 g/mL, what is the mass of 23 mL of nitric acid?

_____

5. The Hope diamond has a mass of 9.1 g. Diamonds have a density of 3.614 g/cm³. What is the volume of the Hope diamond?

_____

EXERCISE

2·10

Express the following numbers in scientific notation.

1. 456 m   _____

2. 0.0086 kg   _____

3. 10,000,000 μL   _____

4. 2000 cm   _____

5. 0.0000000075 Tg   _____

EXERCISE
2·11

How many significant figures are in each of the following measurements?

1. 300,000,000 mm   _____

2. 0.750 L   _____

3. 800.0 g   _____

Still stymied by significant figures? Try this little trick. Look at Figure 2.5 and ask yourself these questions:

1. Where is the Pacific Ocean?

2. Where is the Atlantic Ocean?

3. When looking at the number, is the decimal point present or absent?

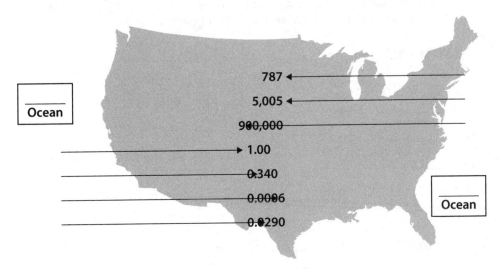

Figure 2.5

Next use the following tips to determine significant numbers:

- If the decimal point is absent (not written), draw an arrow from the Atlantic Ocean until you touch a nonzero number (1, 2, 3, 4, 5, 6, 7, 8, or 9). Any digit that your line does *not* go through is *significant*.

    Since 787 has three digits that you did *not* cross through, it has three significant figures.

    5,005, which has 0s that are trapped between two nonzero digits, has four digits that are not crossed through, so it has four significant figures.

    For the number 900,000, you crossed through five 0s, leaving only the one 9 not marked through—so 900,000 has one significant figure.

- If the decimal point is present (written), draw an arrow from the Pacific Ocean until you touch a nonzero number. Again, any digit that your line does *not* cross through is a significant figure.

    For the number 1.00, the arrow stops at the 1. No digits are crossed through, so 1.00 has three significant figures.

For the number 0.340, only the 0 to the left of the decimal point is crossed through, so 0.340 has three significant figures.

In the number 0.0006, the decimal point is present and the arrow is drawn all the way to the 6. All four 0s are crossed through—only the 6 remains—so 0.0006 has one significant figure.

In the last example, 0.0290, the first two 0s are crossed through when the arrow stops at the 2, leaving the 2, the 9, and the last 0 unmarked. Therefore 0.0290 has three significant figures.

With this little trick, all the different types of 0s have been addressed: trapped, trailing without a decimal point, trailing with a decimal point, and leading. Hopefully this will help you determine which digits are significant in a measurement.

EXERCISE
2·12

Determine how many significant figures are in each of the calculations below. Remember that the number of significant figures in a measurement does not always determine how many significant figures there are in your answer. Next, complete the calculation, rounding the answer so that it has the correct number of significant figures.

1. 45.6 g + 0.234 g + 0.87 g = _____

   45.6 g has _____ sig figs.

   0.234 g has _____ sig figs.

   0.87 has _____ sig figs.

2. 1,808 mL − 5.00 mL = _____

   1,808 mL has _____ sig figs.

   5.00 mL has _____ sig figs.

3. 0.00685 km × 0.0007 km = _____

   0.00685 km has _____ sig figs.

   0.0007 km has _____ sig figs.

4. 9,040,000 m ÷ 35,000 s = _____

   9,040,000 m has _____ sig figs.

   35,000 s has _____ sig figs.

5. $\dfrac{5.36\,g}{(4.5\,mL - 2.2\,mL)}$ = _____

   5.36 g has _____ sig figs.

   4.5 mL has _____ sig figs.

   2.2 mL has _____ sig figs.

Draw the indicated number of shots on each target that best represents the given description.

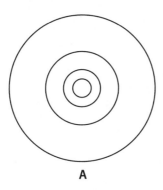
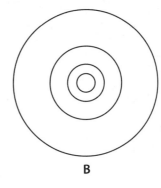

A   B

1. On target A, draw one shot that is accurate.

2. On target B, draw five shots that are neither accurate nor precise.

Complete the following conversions.

1. How many seconds are in 12.0 hr?

_____

2. How many liters are in 0.50 μ?

_____

3. How many nanometers are in 5 km?

_____

4. How many m/s are in 120 km/hr?

_____

5. How many g/mL are in 0.00486 kg/m³?
   (For this problem use the conversions
   1 mL = 1 cm³ and 1,000,000 cm³ = 1 m³.)

_____

Atomic structure and nuclear reactions

Atomic structure

Even though there are many tiny subatomic particles, in general the chemist is concerned with the electrons, protons, and neutrons. The concept of the atom and its structure has undergone many changes through time. The term *atom* was introduced by Democritus, who lived between 460 and 370 B.C. He stated atoms were indestructible and indivisible, and differed only in size, shape, and motion. The main philosophers of the time—including Aristotle—disagreed with Democritus. They argued instead there were four elements (earth, air, water, and fire) with four qualities (dryness, hotness, coldness, and moistness), and also two forces: conflict and harmony. The concept of the atom was set aside until John Dalton (1766–1844) reintroduced it. Dalton stated that:

- *Elements* are made of small particles called atoms.
- *Atoms* of the same element are identical, with the same size, mass, and properties.
- *Compounds* are composed of atoms of different elements combined in a set ratio to each other.
- A *chemical reaction* involves rearranging the atoms.

As further experiments were done, ideas about the atom underwent revision. The charged particles were found first—the electron (by J. J. Thomson in 1897) and the proton (by Ernest Rutherford in 1919). The last particle discovered was the neutron (by James Chadwick in 1932). Thomson used cathode-ray tubes to find electron particles deflected by an electric field, and he also found the charge-to-mass ratio of the electron. Robert Millikan in 1909 did an oil-drop experiment and established the elementary electric charge of a single electron. At first Thomson hypothesized these particles were throughout the atom, like plums in pudding (plum-pudding model). In another experiment called the gold-foil experiment, Rutherford was astonished to discover the atom had a *nucleus* composed of a concentrated positive charge, with the electrons outside the nucleus in an area that was mostly empty space. This experiment changed the model of the atom to the current basic structure. Other experiments were done by Neils Bohr, and theories were developed to explain how the electrons were arranged in the atom. The Bohr model of the hydrogen atom proposed that electrons orbit the nucleus. Later, parts of the Bohr model were found to be incorrect and other models were developed, which will be explored in Chapter 4. From these experiments and ideas, the basic structure of the atom has been determined.

The basic particles of the atom found in the nucleus are the *proton* and *neutron*. The *electron* is found outside the nucleus in shaped electron clouds called *orbitals*. We will look closely at electron orbitals in Chapter 4. The mass of a proton and the mass of a neutron are almost equal to each other and are each considered to be approximately 1.0 amu (atomic mass unit). The electron's mass is extremely small in comparison (1/1840 amu).

For any element, the *atomic number* is the number of protons in any atom of that element. It defines the element. How can there be different atoms of the same element? All atoms of an element have the same number of protons, but they can have different numbers of neutrons. (This is like all the members of a family having the same last name but different first names.) These atoms with different numbers of neutrons are called *isotopes* of the element.

Since an atom is not charged, the number of electrons (e^-) in an atom will be equal to the number of protons (p^+). The positive charge of the protons is cancelled by the negative charge of the electrons: $p^+ - e^- = 0$. If the number of protons and the number of electrons are not equal, the particle is called an ion. If the ion is positively charged—due to its having more protons than electrons—it is called a cation. An example is the lithium cation, with three protons and two electrons resulting in a positive charge of 1: $3^+ - 2^- = 1^+$. This is written as Li^+. If the ion is negatively charged, due to its having more electrons than protons, it is called an anion. For instance, the oxide anion has eight protons and 10 electrons, resulting in a charge of 2 negative: $8^+ - 10^- = 2^-$. This is written as O^{2-}.

> Note that when the charge is only 1, the 1 is not included in the symbol; when it is greater than 1, then the integer is included. Charges are always integers—one-half or other fractions of an electron or proton do not exist.

How are the number of neutrons calculated? Each isotope has a *mass number*, an integer which is equal to the number of protons plus the number of neutrons. The mass number (A) minus the atomic number (Z) equals the number of neutrons (n^0): $A - Z = n^0$. For example, uranium-238, also written as $^{238}_{92}U$, has a mass number of 238 (the sum of the protons and neutrons is at the top left of the isotope notation) and an atomic number of 92 (the atomic number, which is the number of protons, is found at the bottom left of the isotope notation); the number of neutrons is therefore 238 minus 92, or 146. The isotope notation then sets up nicely as a subtraction problem, with the mass on top and the number of protons below:

$$\begin{array}{r} 238 \\ -92 \\ \hline =146 \end{array}$$

Sometimes the bottom number—the atomic number—is not given in the notation, since it is understood based on the given element symbol. *All* atoms of uranium (U) have an atomic number of 92. If you know the element, you can find the number of protons by looking for the atomic number on the periodic table. For instance, ^{63}Cu has a mass number of 63 and has an atomic number of 29, therefore $63 - 29 = 34$ neutrons. The following table has additional examples for reference. Notice that the charge on the ion does *not* change the number of neutrons or protons, only the number of electrons.

Element isotope/ ion symbol	Proton number	Neutron number	Electron number	Atom or ion
lead-208	82	$208 - 82 = 126$	82	atom
$^{32}S^{2-}$	16	$32 - 16 = 16$	$16 + x = -2; x = 18$	ion (anion)
$^{30}Ca^{2+}$	20	$40 - 20 = 20$	$20 + x = 2; x = 18$	ion (cation)

Complete the following table using the information given and the periodic table at the end of the book.

PARTICLE	MASS #	ATOMIC #	# OF p^+	# OF n^0	# OF e^-
1. Phosphorus-31	___	___	___	___	___
2. Cobalt-60	___	___	___	___	___
3. ___	14	6	___	___	6
4. ___	___	___	17	20	18
5. Calcium-43	___	___	20	___	___
6. ___	___	94	___	148	94
7. ___	50	24	___	___	24
8. ___	65	29	___	___	27
9. ^{15}N	___	___	___	___	___
10. $^{34}S^{2-}$	___	___	___	___	___

EXERCISE
3·2

Answer the following questions.

1. What is the isotope notation for phosphorus-31? _____

2. What is the isotope notation for cobalt-60? _____

3. What is the isotope notation for the particle in question 3 in Exercise 3-1? _____

4. What is the isotope notation for the particle in question 4 in Exercise 3-1? _____

5. Write the isotope notation for an isotope with a mass of 211 and a Z of 82. _____

6. An isotope has an A of 46 and a Z of 22. Write the notation for this isotope. _____

7. Write the isotope notation of an atom with a Z of 86 and an A of 222. _____

8. Write the isotope notation for magnesium-25. _____

9. What is the isotope notation for iridium-191? _____

10. What is the isotope notation for neon-22? _____

Average mass

All elements have isotopes. Every hydrogen atom has one proton, no matter which isotope of hydrogen it is. Hydrogen-1, or ^1H, has one proton and no neutrons; it is often referred to as protium. Hydrogen-2, or ^2H, has one proton and one neutron; it is often referred to as deuterium. Hydrogen-3, or ^3H, has one proton and two neutrons and is often referred to as tritium.

So why isn't the mass of hydrogen on the periodic table given as 1, 2, or 3? The mass on the table is the average mass of a sample of the element, which takes into account its isotopic mass times the percentage of occurrence (or percent abundance) in the sample, written as a decimal. From the hydrogen mass of 1.008 on the periodic table, we can see that hydrogen-1 is the most abundant isotope, since the average is extremely close to 1 amu! For hydrogen, any sample will contain 99.9885% hydrogen-1, 0.0115% hydrogen-2, and only a trace of hydrogen-3. It is also true that the protons and neutrons do not each have an exact mass of 1, and that when a nucleus is formed some of the mass of the components (protons and neutrons are collectively called "nucleons") is released as energy according to Einstein's famous equation $E = mc^2$. So there are three reasons why actual atomic masses are *not* whole numbers and are not equal to an element's mass number.

For copper there are two stable isotopes in nature: copper-63 and copper-65. Cu-63 occurs at 69.17% and Cu-65 at 30.83% and they add to 100.00%. To find the average mass, the percentages must first be converted to decimal form. Using the formula of mass times the decimal abundance for each isotope and then adding the results together, we get $(63 \times 0.6917) + (65 \times 0.3083) = 63.62$ amu. An atomic mass unit has a mass of 1.9×10^{-23} g. This means the atomic mass found on the periodic table is *not* the mass in grams of an atom! (There will be more about this later, in Chapter 7.) To find the mass in grams of one atom, the mass in amu would be multiplied by the ratio $\frac{1.9 \times 10^{-23} \text{ g}}{1 \text{ amu}}$.

EXERCISE

3·3

Calculate the atomic mass of each of the following elements using the percent abundances given for each isotope.

1. Magnesium-24   78.99

    Magnesium-25   10.00

    Magnesium-26   11.01

_____

_____

2. Bromine-79   50.69

    Bromine-81   49.31

_____

_____

3. Platinum-190   0.0140

    Platinum-192   0.782

    Platinum-194   32.967

    Platinum-195   33.832

    Platinum-196   25.242

    Platinum-198   7.163

_____

_____

4. Iridium-191   37.58

    Iridium-193   62.42

_____

_____

5. Chromium-50   4.35

    Chromium-52   83.80

    Chromium-53   9.500

    Chromium-54   2.350

_____

_____

Nuclear reactions

If atoms of an element can have different masses due to differing numbers of neutrons, are they all stable? No; they may be the same element, but some forms are unstable and undergo *radioactive decay*. In radioactive decay, the nucleus of the atom changes its particle arrangement. The main decay particles are the *alpha particle, beta particle* (electron), and *neutron*. The emission of a *gamma ray* is often observed during radioactive decay. A gamma ray is not a particle but high-energy electromagnetic radiation.

Nuclear reactions allow atoms to change from one element to another when protons are lost or gained. Remember, the number of protons determines the element's identity—so if a proton is lost or gained, the identity of the element has changed! These are the only reactions that can change an element. A summary of the main radioactive particles follows.

- An alpha particle is a helium nucleus composed of two protons and two neutrons. The symbol is either $_2^4\text{He}$ or $_2^4\alpha$. It has a charge of positive 2, as it has no electrons, so it can also be written $^4\text{He}^{2+}$.

    Due to the loss of two protons, an alpha decay causes the original element to turn into the element two before it on the periodic table. The mass number of the element will go down by four due to the loss of two neutrons and two protons.

◆ A beta particle, β, is an electron from the nucleus, resulting from the transformation of a neutron into a proton and an electron. The electron is emitted from the nucleus and the proton remains. The complete symbol is $_{-1}^{0}\beta$.

A beta decay causes the element turn into the element one beyond it on the periodic table due to the increase of one proton. The mass of the element will not change, since the loss of one neutron is compensated by the gain of one proton.

◆ A neutron has a mass number of 1 and no proton. The symbol is $_{0}^{1}n$.

A neutron decay does not change the element's identity, since no protons are involved. The loss of a neutron does reduce the mass number by one.

Nuclear equations

A nuclear reaction can be represented through a balanced nuclear equation. In a nuclear equation, a tracking system for the particles in the nucleus is used. Due to *conservation of mass*, the atomic numbers (number of protons) and mass numbers (protons plus neutrons) on the left-hand side of the equation must equal the numbers on the right-hand side. In the following equation for the alpha decay of polonium-212, the total mass on both sides is equal (212 = 4 + 208) and the number of protons is equal (84 = 2 + 82). The symbol of the element is *not* the same, since the number of protons has changed. The equation is:

$$_{84}^{212}Po \rightarrow {}_{2}^{4}\alpha + {}_{82}^{208}Pb$$

In the following equation for the beta decay of carbon-14, the total mass on both sides is equal (14 = 0 + 14) and the number of protons is equal (6 = −1 + 7). The nuclear equation is:

$$_{6}^{14}C \rightarrow {}_{-1}^{0}\beta + {}_{7}^{14}N$$

Decay series and stability

Many elements do not reach stability in just one decay step, but must go through a series of decay steps to reach a stable state. One factor influencing this is the neutron-to-proton ratio. For elements with an atomic number less than 20, a stable configuration is a 1:1 ratio of neutrons to protons. Look above at the carbon-14 beta decay. It has an 8:6 ratio before decay, but a 7:7 ratio—which is 1:1—after the beta decay!

What about elements with an atomic number above 20? In general, nuclei with an even number of protons and neutrons are more stable than those with an odd number. For elements with an atomic number greater than 20 the number of neutrons will be greater than the number of protons. All elements above atomic number 83 are radioactive and undergo decay. Figure 3.1 shows the beginning of the uranium-238 decay series. Each part of the series takes a different amount of time. This means in an old sample containing uranium, such as a rock, several different members of the series will be found.

Uranium-238 alpha decay

- $^{238}_{92}\text{U} \rightarrow {}^{4}_{2}\alpha + {}^{234}_{90}\text{Th}$

Thorium-234 beta decay

- $^{234}_{90}\text{Th} \rightarrow {}^{0}_{-1}\beta + {}^{234}_{91}\text{Pa}$

Protactinium-234 beta decay

- $^{234}_{91}\text{Pa} \rightarrow {}^{0}_{-1}\beta + {}^{234}_{92}\text{U}$

Uranium-234 alpha decay

- $^{234}_{92}\text{U} \rightarrow {}^{4}_{2}\alpha + {}^{230}_{90}\text{Th}$

| 238U |

| 234Th |

| 234Pa |

| 234U |

| 230Th |

This continues for six more alpha and four more beta decays until stable lead-206 is formed.

$^{230}_{90}\text{Th} \rightarrow 6\,{}^{4}_{2}\alpha + 4\,{}^{0}_{-1}\beta + {}^{206}_{82}\text{Pb}$

| 206Pb |

Figure 3.1

Supply the missing particle in each of the following steps, beginning with the second reaction of the neptunium decay series.

1. $^{241}_{94}Pu \rightarrow$ _____ $+ ^{0}_{-1}\beta$

2. $^{241}_{95}Am \rightarrow ^{237}_{93}Np +$ _____

3. _____ $\rightarrow ^{233}_{91}Pa + ^{4}_{2}\alpha$

4. $^{233}_{91}Pa \rightarrow ^{233}_{92}U +$ _____

5. $^{233}_{92}U \rightarrow$ _____ $+ ^{4}_{2}He$

6. $^{229}_{90}Th \rightarrow ^{225}_{88}Ra +$ _____

7. $^{225}_{88}Ra -$ _____ $+ ^{0}_{-1}\beta$

8. _____ $\rightarrow ^{221}_{87}Fr + ^{4}_{2}He$

9. $^{221}_{87}Fr \rightarrow$ _____ $+ ^{4}_{2}He$

10. _____ $\rightarrow ^{213}_{83}Bi + ^{4}_{2}He$

11. _____ $\rightarrow ^{209}_{81}Tl + ^{4}_{2}He$

12. $^{209}_{81}Tl \rightarrow$ _____ $+ ^{0}_{-1}\beta$

13. $^{209}_{82}Pb \rightarrow$ _____ $+ ^{0}_{-1}\beta$

As mentioned above, the length of a step in a decay series varies. The length of time it takes half of a sample to decay is called its half-life. Does this mean that at the half-life time half of the sample changes? No! The sample is constantly undergoing change. If half of a sample has decayed in one half-life, how much is left after two half-lives? Half of the remaining half is one-quarter, or 25%. The third half-life will lose one-half of the remaining one-quarter, which is one-eighth. The following table shows these relationships.

Half-life	1	2	3	4	5
Fraction lost	$\frac{1}{2}$	$\frac{3}{4}$	$\frac{7}{8}$	$\frac{15}{16}$	$\frac{31}{32}$
Fraction left	$\frac{1}{2}$	$\frac{1}{4}$	$\frac{1}{8}$	$\frac{1}{16}$	$\frac{1}{32}$
Percentage lost	50%	75%	87.5%	93.75%	96.875%
Percentage left	50%	25%	12.5%	6.25%	3.125%

How much of a 50.0 g sample will be left after two half-lives? 50.0 g times 0.25 = 12.5 g. Another problem might be to find out how long it takes a sample to go through a half-life. If a sample loses 75% in 12 days, two half-lives have occurred; 12 days divided by 2 = 6 days per half-life.

The above may be confusing, because if you were to weigh the 50.0 g sample it would still weigh 50.0 g after many half-lives! Why? Every decay produces a product atom, usually called the *daughter atom*. The *production* of daughter atoms will be the amount calculated to be lost by the parent sample. So the mass of *daughter* atoms in the 50.0 g sample above will be 25.0 grams after one half-life, 37.5 g after two half-lives, and so on. The tiny mass lost in the form of energy emitted is too small to measure on an ordinary balance. Scientists can use the relative amounts of parent and daughter atoms in a sample to estimate the age of certain materials. If the sample has equal percentages of parent to daughter atoms, this may mean the sample is one half-life old, assuming all the daughter atoms were formed after the sample was made.

The main problem scientists face in estimating age this way is deciding whether the number of daughter atoms was really zero when the sample was made, and whether any could have been lost from the sample during its lifetime. Some "dating" methods can look at just the amount of parent left, since it is known how much would have been in the sample when it was formed. This is true for the method using ^{14}C decay, since all living systems contain the same ratio of ^{14}C to ^{12}C.

When the death of a living thing occurs, only the ^{14}C decays, with a half-life of 5,700 years. A wood sample from a ring in a dead tree is 5,700 years old if it has one-half of the ratio of ^{14}C to ^{12}C that it had when it was alive. The daughter product from the decay, ^{14}N, is not measured.

EXERCISE
3·5

Solve the following problems.

1. Francium-221 has a half-life of 4.8 min. What percentage of the sample is left after 19.2 min?

2. If the sample in question 1 had started with 250 g of francium-221, how many grams of the sample would be left after 19.2 min?

3. A 400 g sample of plutonium-241 decays until 50 g remain. The time that has elapsed is 43.2 y. What is the half-life of plutonium-241?

4. How many years would it take for a 100 g sample of radium-226 to decay to 3.125 g if the half-life of radium-226 is 1,600 y?

5. The half-life of ^{71}Zn is 2.4 min. How long will it take to decay to one thirty-second of its mass?

6. The half-life of the radiotracer ^{24}Na is 4.0 days. How long will it take the sample to decay to one-sixteenth of its mass?

7. If a sample starts with 6.54×10^{12} atoms of ^{131}I, with a half-life of 8.07 days, how many atoms will be left after four half-lives?

_____

_____

8. If a sample decays to one-eighth of its mass in 21 days, what is its half-life?

_____

_____

9. If a sample starts with 1.97×10^{17} atoms of strontium-90, with a half-life of 28 years, how many atoms of strontium-90 will remain after 140 years?

_____

_____

10. The plutomium-238 in pacemakers has a half-life of 27 years. If the original sample has 3.94×10^{10} atoms of the isotope, how many will remain after 81 years?

_____

_____

Which scientist did each of the following?

1. Conducted the oil-drop experiment _____

2. Conducted the cathode-ray experiments _____

3. Conducted the gold-foil experiment _____

4. Discovered the electron's charge-to-mass ratio _____

5. Described the plum-pudding model _____

6. Discovered the nucleus _____

7. Developed the model of electron arrangement in the hydrogen atom _____

8. Discovered the neutron _____

Complete the following table describing subatomic particles.

	PARTICLE	SYMBOL	CHARGE	MASS (IN AMU)	LOCATION
1.	Proton	_____	_____	_____	_____
2.	_____	e⁻	_____	_____	_____
3.	_____	_____	neutral	1	_____

Which nuclear-reaction component or components (alpha particle, beta, or gamma ray) does each of the following statements describe?

1. Has a mass number of four   _____

2. Has a mass number of zero   _____

3. Has two protons   _____

4. Has no protons   _____

5. Has no particles   _____

6. Has a charge of 2⁺   _____

7. Has two neutrons   _____

8. Is a wave of energy   _____

9. Has a charge of 1⁺   _____

10. Has no neutrons   _____

Supply the missing particle in each of the following nuclear equations.

1. $^{139}Ba \rightarrow {}^{139}La + $ _____

2. _____ $+ {}_{-1}^{0}e^- \rightarrow {}_{91}^{233}Pa$

3. $^{3}_{1}H + {}_{1}^{2}H \rightarrow {}_{2}^{2}He + $ _____

4. $^{235}U + {}_{0}^{1}n \rightarrow {}_{38}^{90}Sr + $ _____

5. $^{22}Na + {}_{-1}^{0}e^- \rightarrow $ _____

Write balanced nuclear equations for the following reactions.

6. Radon-198 undergoes alpha decay

_____

_____

7. Platinum-199 undergoes beta decay

_____

_____

8. Iridium-174 undergoes alpha decay

_____

_____

9. Seaborgium-263 undergoes alpha decay

_____

_____

10. Gold-211 undergoes beta decay

_____

_____

The periodic table, periodicity, and periodic trends

·4·

Historical background

The main organizing "tool" for the chemist is the *Periodic Table*. Understanding the construction of the table will allow you to unlock many of the components of chemistry. There have been and continue to be many different versions of the periodic table, however there is a version that has been accepted by the international chemistry community. Dmitri Mendeleev, Henry Moseley, and Glenn Seaborg, along with many others, contributed to the development of the current periodic table. Although the basic structure has not changed recently, the table is still expanding as new elements are synthesized, isolated, and identified.

Mendeleev arranged the known elements of his time by increasing atomic mass, included columns of repeating properties, attributed apparent problems with this structure to incorrect masses, and predicted the properties of four elements: scandium, technetium, gallium, and germanium (see Table 4.1).

Moseley changed the table to an arrangement where the elements were in order by increasing proton number instead of mass, thus fixing the issues in Mendeleev's table, and Seaborg moved the lanthanides and actinides from the body of the table to the rows below the table and started adding new elements in correct locations.

Thus as our knowledge of the elements has expanded, the arrangement of the periodic table has undergone revision. Although the history of chemistry is interesting, the focus of this chapter is understanding what we now know. Does the periodic table look the same worldwide? Yes. Although the names of the elements may differ in different languages, the symbols are universal. Cl represents the same element, whether scientists in the United States call it *chlorine* or those in France call it *chlore*.

The arrangements

The periodic table has columns and rows. The columns are called *families* or *groups*, and the rows are called *periods*. Different variations of the periodic table's column-numbering system exist. Which one should be used? The system used by the *IUPAC*—the International Union of Pure and Applied Chemistry—is the standard. If any questions arise about accepted formats of the periodic table, you should look at these standards; they can be found in a current edition of the *CRC Handbook of Chemistry and Physics*.

Table 4.1 A Rendering of Mendeleev's 1872 Periodic Table

Tabelle II

Reihen	Gruppe I	Gruppe II	Gruppe III	Gruppe IV	Gruppe V	Gruppe VI	Gruppe VII	Gruppe VIII
				RH^4	RH^3	RH^2	RH	—
	R^2O	RO	R^2O^3	RO^2	R^2O^5	RO^3	R^2O^7	RO^4
1	H = 1							
2	Li = 7	Be = 9,4	B = 11	C = 12	N = 14	O = 16	F = 19	
3	Na = 23	Mg = 24	Al = 27,3	Si = 28	P = 31	S = 32	Cl = 35,5	
4	K = 39	Ca = 40	— = 44	Ti = 48	V = 51	Cr = 52	Mn = 55	Fe = 56, Co = 59, Ni = 59, Cu = 63
5	(Cu = 63)	Zn = 65	— = 68	— = 72	As = 75	Se = 78	Br = 80	
6	Rb = 85	Sr = 87	?Yt = 88	Zr = 90	Nb = 94	Mo = 96	— = 100	Ru = 104, Rh = 104, Pd = 106, Ag = 108
7	(Ag = 108)	Cd = 112	In = 113	Sn = 118	Sb = 122	Te = 125	J = 127	
8	Cs = 133	Ba = 137	?Di = 138	?Ce = 140	—	—	—	_____
9	(—)	—	—	—	—	—	—	
10	—	—	?Er = 178	?La = 180	Ta = 182	W = 184	—	Os = 195, Ir = 197, Pt = 198, Au = 199
11	(Au = 199)	Hg = 200	Tl = 204	Pb = 207	Bi = 208	—	—	_____
12	—	—	—	Th = 231	—	U = 240	—	_____

Note: *Gruppe* means "group" and *Reihen* means "row." Also in the table, below the group labels, are the predicted formulas with hydrogen and with oxygen for each group. Notice that the accepted format during that period was to use a superscript instead of a subscript for the number of each atom in the formula. Masses given without symbols indicate elements not known at the time but predicted by Mendeleev. His predictions were later proved correct and identified as scandium, gallium, and germanium.

The periodic table is composed of elements found as solids, liquids, and gases at room temperature, as shown in Figure 4.1. Elements are also classified as metals, metalloids (also called semimetals), and nonmetals, as in Figure 4.2.

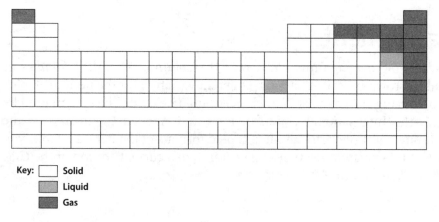

Key: ☐ Solid
　　 ☐ Liquid
　　 ■ Gas

Figure 4.1

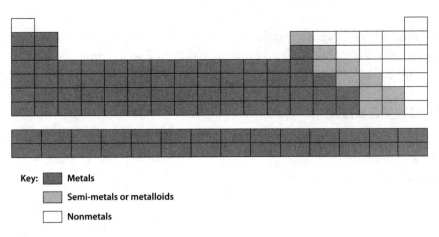

Key:
- ■ Metals
- ▨ Semi-metals or metalloids
- □ Nonmetals

Figure 4.2

EXERCISE

4·1

Complete the following chart using the periodic table at the end of the book.

ELEMENT	METAL, METALLOID, OR NONMETAL	SOLID, LIQUID, OR GAS (AT ROOM TEMP.)	COLUMN #	PERIOD #
1. Oxygen	————	————	————	————
2. Silicon	————	————	————	————
3. Mercury	————	————	————	————
4. ————	————	————	2	6
5. ————	————	————	18	2
6. ————	————	————	17	4
7. Francium	————	————	————	————
8. Radon	————	————	————	————
9. Germanium	————	————	————	————

The arrangements in the table are like a code. They can tell us a lot of things about a substance. Why do elements exist in different states? This can be explained by looking at their structure and the forces holding them together.

The current periodic table has elements arranged by increasing atomic number. Remember, the atomic number represents the number of protons in the element. The atomic number increases by one moving from left to right across the periodic table. Hydrogen is element 1 and has one proton; helium is element 2 and has two protons; lithium is element 3 and has three protons; and so on.

The electrons determine how reactive an element is. The founders of the periodic table arranged the elements based on common characteristics. As more information about the location, function, and movement of electrons was discovered, it was found that how these properties change throughout the table is linked to the electronic structure of the atom.

Each electronic structure has a set of properties that relate to one another. The periods all fill electrons into the same energy levels in four different types of shaped areas, called *orbitals*. The columns fill the same number of electrons into the same type of orbital but at a different average

The periodic table, periodicity, and periodic trends **41**

distance from the nucleus, and so at different energy levels. The first column, group 1, has one electron in its outermost orbital, which is an *s* orbital. Column 2—i.e., group 2—has two electrons in the outermost *s* orbital. The arrangement of orbitals and order of filling is important to understand.

Orbital arrangement

The orbitals are designated by the symbols *s*, *p*, *d*, and *f*: *s* has one orbital at each energy level (Figure 4.3), *p* has three orbitals (Figure 4.4), *d* has five orbitals (Figure 4.5), and *f* has seven orbitals (Figure 4.6).

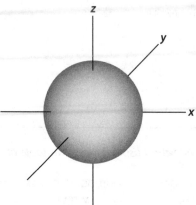

Figure 4.3

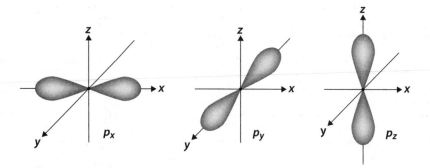

Figure 4.4

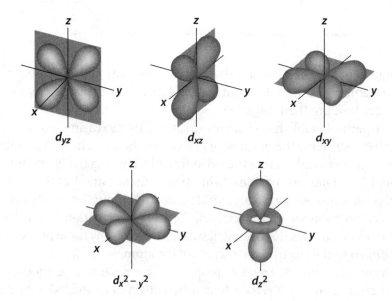

Figure 4.5

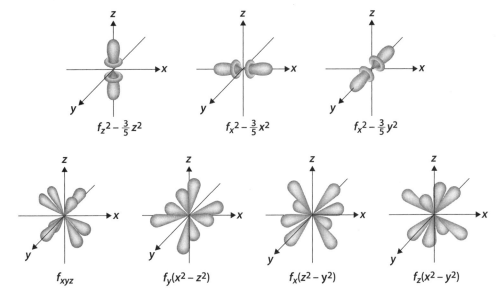

$f_{z^2 - \frac{3}{5}z^2}$ $f_{x^2 - \frac{3}{5}x^2}$ $f_{x^2 - \frac{3}{5}y^2}$

f_{xyz} $f_{y(x^2 - z^2)}$ $f_{x(z^2 - y^2)}$ $f_{z(x^2 - y^2)}$

Figure 4.6

Each individual orbital can hold two electrons. Knowing each orbital can contain a specific number of electrons, the one orbital of *s* can contain a maximum of 2 electrons, the three orbitals of *p* can hold 6 electrons, the five orbitals of *d* can hold 10 electrons, and the seven orbitals of *f* can hold 14 electrons. Which orbital is being filled to form an element can be recognized from the periodic table (see Figure 4.7).

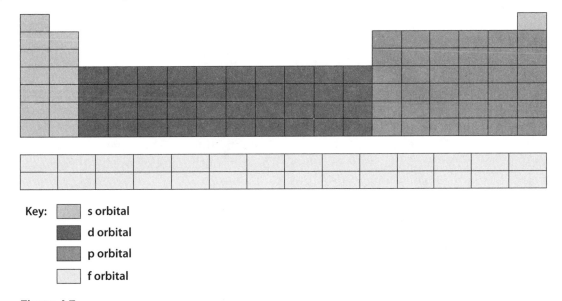

Key: □ s orbital
      ■ d orbital
      ■ p orbital
      □ f orbital

Figure 4.7

Each orbital has a different energy, and they fill in a particular order. If one knows the number of electrons an atom has, the electron configuration can be written. The electron configuration is a notation indicating all the electrons in the atom and where they are located. This notation gives the energy level of the orbital the electron is in, the type of orbital, and the number of electrons. The energy level is indicated by an integer from one to seven, the orbitals each have a letter—*s, p, d,* or *f*—and the number of electrons varies by the type of orbital, with an upper limit given by this list:

s orbital   ◆ 1 orbital
              ◆ 2 electrons (maximum)

p orbital	◆ 3 orbitals	
	◆ 6 electrons (maximum)	
d orbital	◆ 5 orbitals	
	◆ 10 electrons (maximum)	
f orbital	◆ 7 orbitals	
	◆ 14 electrons (maximum)	

The order of filling follows the order shown in Figure 4.8: 1s, 2s, 2p, 3s, 3p, 4s, 3d, 4p, 5s, 4d, 5p, 6s, 4f, 5d, 6p, 7s, 5f, 6d, and 7p. You can see that these designations follow the order of increasing atomic number on the periodic table. Note that these designations are *not* included on most standard periodic tables.

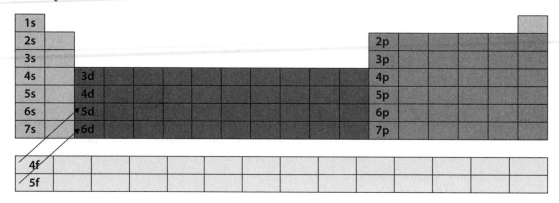

Figure 4.8

Electron configurations

The order that electrons fill orbitals in follows the *Aufbau principle*: Electrons fill orbitals from lowest energy (most stable) to highest energy. For example, magnesium, symbol Mg, has 12 protons and as a neutral atom has 12 electrons. Those electrons are in 1s, 2s, 2p, and 3s. When this is written as $1s^2 2s^2 2p^6 3s^2$, it is called an electron configuration. The superscripts are the number of electrons in the particular type of orbital. The sum of the superscripts will equal the number of electrons in the atom or ion. In this case, $2 + 2 + 6 + 2 = 12$!

Atom	Number of electrons	Electron configuration
Calcium	20	$1s^2 2s^2 2p^6 3s^2 3p^6 4s^2$
Iron	26	$1s^2 2s^2 2p^6 3s^2 3p^6 4s^2 3d^6$
Tin	50	$1s^2 2s^2 2p^6 3s^2 3p^6 4s^2 3d^{10} 4p^6 5s^2 4d^{10} 5p^2$

EXERCISE
4·2

Write electron configurations for the following elements.

1. Carbon _____

2. Zinc _____

3. Bromine _____

4. Cesium _____

5. Bismuth _____

6. Potassium _____

7. Manganese _____

8. Iodine _____

9. Cadmium _____

10. Lead _____

11. Francium _____

12. Platinum _____

13. Titanium _____

14. Oxygen _____

15. Beryllium _____

When orbitals are grouped by their first number—called the *principal quantum number*—the order changes to 1s, 2s, 2p, 3s, 3p, 3d, 4s, 4p, 4d, 4f, 5s, 5p, 5d, 5f, etc. By placing the orbitals in this order, it is easier identify what are called the *valence*, or outermost, electrons. Knowing the number of outer electrons will be vital when drawing structures, as only valence electrons are included. It is also important because when an atom forms a positively charged ion by losing electrons, the electrons lost are from the outermost orbital, *not necessarily the last one filled*. In contrast, when electrons are added to form negatively charged ions, they fill the last orbital being filled.

When Mg $1s^2 2s^2 2p^6 3s^2$ forms the ion Mg^{2+}, the two electrons lost are the 3s electrons, leaving $1s^2 2s^2 2p^6$. Sulfur (S), element 16, has 16 electrons, resulting in the configuration of $1s^2 2s^2 2p^6 3s^2 3p^4$. To form sulfur's 2negative ion, S^{2-}, two electrons must be added to the configuration, forming $1s^2 2s^2 2p^6 3s^2 3p^6$.

EXERCISE
4·3

Write the electron configurations for the following atoms and their corresponding ions.

1. Lithium and Li+ _____
_____

2. Aluminum and Al³⁺ _____
_____

3. Lead and Pb⁴⁺ _____
_____

4. Nitrogen and N³⁻ _____
_____

5. Chlorine and Cl⁻ _____
_____

6. Oxygen and O^{2-} _____

_____

7. Sodium and Na^+ _____

_____

8. Arsenic and As^{5+} _____

_____

9. Fluorine and F^- _____

_____

10. Beryllium and Be^{2+} _____

_____

11. Arsenic and As^{3-} _____

_____

12. Nickel and Ni^{2+} _____

_____

13. Cadmium and Cd^{2+} _____

_____

14. Strontium and Sr^{2+} _____

_____

15. Iron and Fe^{3+} _____

_____

Orbital diagrams

Only two electrons can be in an orbital, and they must have opposite spins. This is called the *Pauli exclusion principle*: no two electrons can be in the same place at the same time with the same spin. While the orbitals fill in order of increasing energy in Aufbau's principle, the order of filling the orbitals follows Hund's rule. Hund's rule states when filling the same type of orbital in the same energy level (*p*, *d*, or *f*) that one electron will go into each orbital before the pairing of electrons will occur. For instance, in the three orbitals of *p*, which we can identify as p_x, p_y, and p_z, the first electron will go into p_x, the second into p_y, the third into p_z, and the fourth will go back to p_x and fill the orbital, the fifth will go into p_y, and the last electron into p_z. The defining of orbitals as px, py, and pz is a convention that allows the model to be built regarding the order of orbital filling as presented here. The first three of the six *p* electrons will all have the same type of spin, and the last three will all have the opposite spin of the first three. This is because this arrangement forms the most stable energy; this rule must be understood as configurations are studied. Look at Figure 4.9, the orbital diagram for nitrogen. The seven electrons in nitrogen are arranged in the configuration $1s^2 2s^2 2p^3$. The three electrons in the *p* orbitals are split among the three orbitals, following Hund's rule. The three p orbitals and their electrons can be written in this case as $2p_x^12p_y^12p_z^1$. This is a more stable configuration than having $2p_x^22p_y^1$ with no $2p_z$ electron.

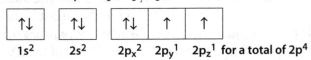

$1s^2 \quad 2s^2 \quad 2p_x^1 \quad 2p_y^1 \quad 2p_z^1$ for a total of $2p^3$

Figure 4.9

In Figure 4.10, the eight electrons of oxygen are in the configuration $1s^22s^22p^4$; the fourth electron in the p cloud goes back to the first orbital and goes opposite in spin. So the p cloud's configuration is written out fully as $2p_x^22p_y^12p_z^1$.

$1s^2 \quad 2s^2 \quad 2p_x^2 \quad 2p_y^1 \quad 2p_z^1$ for a total of $2p^4$

Figure 4.10

EXERCISE
4·4

Draw orbital diagrams for the following elements and ions.

1. Sodium

2. Phosphorus

3. Cobalt

4. Selenium

5. Cadmium

6. Na^+

7. Cd^{2+}

8. O^{2-}

9. P^{3-}

10. Neon

11. Helium

12. Nickel

13. Calcium

14. Ca^{2+}

15. Fe^{3+}

While chemists often describe electrons as "filling orbitals," in fact the electrons *are* the orbitals. An orbital is the probability of an electron being in a certain region around the nucleus. There is nothing there to "fill" until the electron is there! This is just a convenient way for people to describe atoms. So a better description for the subject of the Aufbau principle is "building atoms" rather than "filling orbitals."

Periodic trends

Periodic trends are patterns that can be recognized based on observations of the elements. Two concepts used to describe the reasoning behind different periodic trends are shielding and effective nuclear charge.

Shielding

Orbital diagrams and electron configurations help illustrate the location of electrons to further explain the concepts of shielding and effective nuclear charge. These two concepts will in turn help us understand trends in the periodic table.

Going down a column, the atomic number increases and the outer electron orbitals get farther from the nucleus, as a new principal quantum number must be used.

As an atom adds orbitals, the outer electrons have more inner orbitals between themselves and the pull of all the positive charge from the nucleus. Think of the layers of electrons in between as interference, reducing the effect of the electrical charge of the nucleus. The more layers there are, the more shielding there is. The trend describing how this affects the outer electrons is termed "effective nuclear charge." (See the next section.)

If the atom has a larger radius, this means the outermost electrons are easier to remove, since they are not held as tightly as electrons close to the nucleus (which experience more pull from the positive charge of the nucleus). Distance matters—the coulomb attractive force between opposite charges varies with the distance between the charges according to the formula $1/d^2$!

The greater the period number (principal quantum number), the larger the radius. Magnesium has 12 electrons in the configuration $1s^2 2s^2 2p^6 3s^2$ and calcium has 20 electrons in the configuration $1s^2 2s^2 2p^6 3s^2 3p^6 4s^2$. Both configurations end in s^2 electrons, but calcium has an additional energy level and therefore a larger radius. This larger radius exists both because the electrons can only be accommodated at a greater radial distance *and* because there are more inner electrons that provide more shielding. (More periods mean more shielding, thus making it easier to remove outer electrons.)

> The periodic trend is that atoms have larger radii moving down a column. The reason for this trend is that higher energy orbitals with larger radial distances must be used; this increases the shielding moving down a column and reduces the effective nuclear charge (and hence the attraction of the outermost electrons to the nucleus). The result is that the outer electrons are easier to remove moving down a column.

Effective nuclear charge

Moving across a period is different, since the number of outermost energy levels remains the same. Instead of being reduced due to shielding, the effective nuclear charge is increased as the atomic number increases across a period, since there are more protons being added to the nucleus. This greater number of protons results in a larger positive attraction exerted by the nucleus.

This larger attraction results in the atom having a *smaller* radius as you move across a period, due to the *increased* effective nuclear charge (e.g., potassium has 19 electrons in the configuration $1s^2 2s^2 2p^6 3s^2 3p^6 4s^1$, and calcium has 20 electrons in the configuration $1s^2 2s^2 2p^6 3s^2 3p^6 4s^2$). Both have their outermost electrons in the fourth energy level, but calcium has an additional proton in the nucleus, resulting in a greater effective nuclear charge. This means the calcium atom has a smaller radius than the potassium atom.

The trend is that atoms have smaller radii moving across a period. This is the due to increased effective nuclear charge. The result is that electrons are harder to remove as you move across a period.

EXERCISE
4·5

Choose which atom has the smallest radius from the given group and explain the reasoning behind your choice.

1. Nitrogen and oxygen

_____

2. Potassium and rubidium

_____

3. Sulfur, chlorine, and bromine

_____

4. Strontium, cesium, and barium

_____

5. Rubidium and krypton

_____

6. Calcium and gallium

_____

7. Fluorine and iodine

_____

8. Boron and fluorine

_____

9. Carbon, nitrogen, and silicon

_____

10. Neon, argon, and krypton

_____

Atomic radius versus ionic radius

When ions are formed, what happens to the atom's radius and effective nuclear charge depends on whether the ion is a cation or an anion. Remember that when magnesium $1s^2 2s^2 2p^6 3s^2$ forms the cation Mg^{2+}, the two electrons lost are the 3s electrons, leaving $1s^2 2s^2 2p^6$. An entire energy level has been lost, but the number of protons has not changed! The remaining electrons are held more tightly, due to an increased effective nuclear charge based on the reduced number of electrons. In the magnesium atom, 12 protons were pulling on 12 electrons, compared to the 12 protons that are pulling on the 10 electrons in Mg^{2+}.

> The trend is that cations have smaller radii than their corresponding atoms. The reason for this trend is that cations have lost electrons, changing the ratio from an equal number of protons and electrons to one where there are more protons than electrons. This results in an increased effective nuclear charge, making those electrons more tightly bound and harder to remove.

For anions, the opposite is true. For sulfur, symbol S, which has 16 electrons in the configuration $1s^2 2s^2 2p^6 3s^2 3p^4$, the atom gains two electrons to form S^{2-}, resulting in a configuration of $1s^2 2s^2 2p^6 3s^2 3p^6$. The number of protons in the nucleus has not changed but two electrons have been gained. In the sulfur atom, 16 protons were pulling on 16 electrons, but in the S^{2-} anion, 16 protons are pulling on 18 electrons. This reduction in effective nuclear charge means the ion has a larger radius than its atom.

> The periodic trend here is that anions have larger radii than their corresponding atoms. The reason for this trend is that anions gain electrons, changing the ratio from an equal number of protons and electrons to one where there are more electrons than protons. This results in a decreased effective nuclear charge, making the outer electrons easier to remove.

EXERCISE

4·6

Write the electron configurations for the following atoms and their corresponding ions. Based on the proton-to-electron ratio, determine which member of the pair has a larger radius, and explain your reasoning.

PARTICLES	CONFIGURATIONS	PROTON-TO-ELECTRON RATIOS
1. F	_____	_____
F⁻	_____	_____
Which is larger? Explain.	_____	
2. Al	_____	_____
Al³⁺	_____	_____
Which is larger? Explain.	_____	
3. Fe	_____	_____
Fe²⁺	_____	_____
Which is larger? Explain.	_____	
4. As	_____	_____
As³⁻	_____	_____
Which is larger? Explain.	_____	

5. N   _____   _____

   N^{3-} _____   _____

   Which is larger? Explain. _____

6. O   _____   _____

   O^{2-} _____   _____

   Which is larger? Explain. _____

7. Na   _____   _____

   Na^{+} _____   _____

   Which is larger? Explain. _____

8. Ga   _____   _____

   Ga^{3+} _____   _____

   Which is larger? Explain. _____

9. Cr   _____   _____

   Cr^{6+} _____   _____

   Which is larger? Explain. _____

10. Ca   _____   _____

   Ca^{2+} _____   _____

   Which is larger? Explain. _____

First ionization energy

The amount of energy required to remove an electron from a gaseous atom in its ground state is defined as its first ionization energy. How much energy is needed depends on how much shielding is present and what effective nuclear charge is exhibited. Remember that shielding increases down a column, resulting in electrons not being held as tightly; these electrons are easier to remove, and thus ionization energy decreases.

> The periodic trend is that first ionization energy decreases down a column. The reason for this trend is that more shielding and greater distance between the nucleus and outer electrons result in the electrons not being held as tightly; therefore it takes less energy to remove the outer electrons.

Going across a period from left to right, ionization energy tends to increase, since effective nuclear charge increases. Why "tends to" instead of just "does"? There are two exceptions to this trend, each due to a different reason.

◆ Exception 1: Using period 2, moving from beryllium—in Group 2, with a full 2s orbital—to boron, which has a single electron in the higher-energy 2p orbital, it actually takes less energy to remove the single electron in 2p.

◆ Exception 2: Ionization energy also decreases from Group 15 to Group 16. Look again at Figures 4.9 and 4.10 on page 47. Nitrogen's electrons in the *p* orbitals all have parallel spin, while oxygen has two electrons with opposite spins paired in first *p* orbital and it has two lone electrons with parallel spin in the remaining two *p* orbitals. It takes less energy to remove one of the paired-spin electrons from oxygen.

> For representative elements, ionization energy tends to increase across a period, with slight drops as orbital types change from *s* to *p* and as the three orbitals of *p* move from having one unpaired electron in each orbital to having one orbital with paired electrons. The reason for this trend is that increasing effective nuclear charge across a period results in more energy being needed to remove outer electrons.

To review the trends previously discussed, Figure 4.11 shows the patterns in first ionization energy and atomic radius. Note the directions of the arrows!

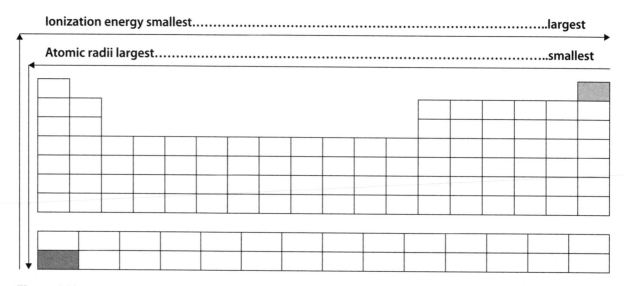

Ionization energy smallest..largest

Atomic radii largest..smallest

Figure 4.11

Choose which atom has the smallest first ionization energy from the given group and explain the reasoning behind your choice. It might be helpful to draw orbital diagrams for the valence electrons of each atom.

1. Carbon and nitrogen

2. Potassium and rubidium

3. Sulfur, selenium, and bromine

4. Rubidium, cesium, and francium

_____

5. Magnesium and aluminum

_____

6. Oxygen and francium

_____

7. Fluorine and nitrogen

_____

8. Helium and neon

_____

9. Boron and gallium

_____

10. Silver and copper

_____

Successive ionization energy

After the energy is added to remove the first electron, adding additional energy can remove additional electrons in sequence. The additional energy to remove each sequential electron is called *successive ionization energy*. The energy required to remove additional electrons is always greater than the first ionization energy, due to the proton-to-electron ratios increasingly favoring the protons as more electrons are removed. Effective nuclear charge increases each time an electron is removed; when an entire energy level is removed, the energy needed increases dramatically as effective nuclear charge on the outer electrons increases dramatically with the smaller radius and the loss of inner shielding. Ionization energies listed in Figure 4.12 are measured in kJ per mole. The concept of a mole will be explained in Chapter 7. The important thing to understand here is that as more electrons are removed, the energy required increases.

	1st electron	2nd electron	3rd electron	4th electron	5th electron
H	1,312				
He	2,373	5,251			
Li	520	7,300	11,815		
Be	899	1,757	14,850	21,005	
B	801	2,430	3,660	25,000	32,820

Figure 4.12

The trend is that successive ionization energies always increase. The reason for this trend is the greater effective nuclear charge that results as electrons are removed, leading to more energy being needed to remove additional electrons.

EXERCISE

4·8

Complete the following chart using the periodic table at the end of the book.

ELEMENT	METAL, METALLOID, OR NONMETAL	SOLID, LIQUID, OR GAS (AT ROOM TEMP.)	COLUMN #	PERIOD #
1. Bromine	________	________	________	________
2. Antimony	________	________	________	________
3. Titanium	________	________	________	________
4. ________	________	________	14	5
5. ________	________	________	17	2
6. ________	________	________	1	1

EXERCISE

4·9

Write electron configurations for the following elements.

1. Krypton ____________________
2. Technetium ____________________
3. Selenium ____________________
4. Barium ____________________
5. Chlorine ____________________

EXERCISE

4·10

Write the electron configurations for the following atoms and their corresponding ions.

1. Cadmium and Cd^{2+} ____________________

____

2. Selenium and Se^{2-} ____________________

____

EXERCISE 4·11

Draw orbital diagrams for the following elements.

1. Beryllium

2. Fluorine

3. Potassium

EXERCISE 4·12

Complete the following chart by filling in each blank with the best choice from the pair of particles. If the values are equal, write "same" in the blank.

	MORE SHIELDING	GREATER EFFECTIVE NUCLEAR CHARGE	LARGER RADIUS	SMALLER IONIZATION ENERGY
1. Li or K	_____	_____	_____	_____
2. Na or Cl	_____	_____	_____	_____
3. K or K⁺	_____	_____	_____	_____
4. Br or Br⁻	_____	_____	_____	_____

Naming compounds and writing formulas

The periodic table will be a big help when it comes to naming compounds and writing formulas. When elements from different parts of the table combine, different types of bonds are made, and the bonding determines the naming system to be used. The possible combinations are metals with metals, metals with nonmetals, nonmetals with nonmetals, and two unique groups: hydrogen with a nonmetal, and carbons primarily with hydrogen. This is like having to learn five foreign languages!

Metal-metal combinations

Metal-metal combinations form metallic bonds. They can conduct electricity in all phases, due to electrons' being available to move in a "sea." Metal-metal solutions are called *alloys*. Alloys go by different names, depending on the identity of the metals and the percentage of each metal in the solution. Other metals or elements can be added to change the properties of an alloy: adding carbon to iron makes steel stronger. Bronze is an alloy of copper and tin, brass is composed of copper and zinc, and steel is an alloy of iron and several other elements, including nickel. Since these are not compounds with exact ratios of atoms, we do not write formulas for them. Their names usually relate to historical developments rather than chemical composition.

Metal-nonmetal combinations

Metal-nonmetal combinations form ionic bonds. The metal combines in the form of a *cation* with the nonmetal in the form of an *anion* (or anion groups) to make a formula unit. The metal cation is always written first in the formula and in the compound name, while the anion is always written second in the formula and in the compound name. Sodium chloride, $NaCl$, is an example of a formula unit that contains an ionic bond. One important cation does not contain a metal atom—it is the ammonium ion, NH_4^+, a group of nonmetal atoms combined with a positive charge. As a cation, ammonium is still written first in a formula.

Writing the formula of a substance that contains ionic bonds from the name

Writing the formula for a chemical compound is an important skill in chemistry. There are certain types of information that are needed to accomplish this task.

- Remember, the cation symbol is always written first in the formula, and the anion symbol is always written second.
- To determine the formula, the charge of each ion must be known (see Table 5.1).

Table 5.1   Selected Ions List

Cation name	Cation symbol	Anion name	Anion symbol
aluminum	Al^{3+}	acetate	$C_2H_3O_2^-$
ammonium	NH_4^+	bromide	Br^-
barium	Ba^{2+}	carbonate	CO_3^{2-}
cadmium	Cd^{2+}	chlorate	ClO_3^-
calcium	Ca^{2+}	chloride	Cl^-
cobalt(II)	Co^{2+}	chromate	CrO_4^{2-}
copper(II)	Cu^{2+}	cyanide	CN^-
copper(I)	Cu^+	dichromate	$Cr_2O_7^{2-}$
hydrogen	H^+	fluoride	F^-
iron(II)	Fe^{2+}	hydride	H^-
iron(III)	Fe^{3+}	bicarbonate	HCO_3^-
lead(II)	Pb^{2+}	hydroxide	OH^-
lead(IV)	Pb^{4+}	iodide	I^-
lithium	Li^+	nitrate	NO_3^-
magnesium	Mg^{2+}	nitride	N^{3-}
nickel(II)	Ni^{2+}	nitrite	NO_2^-
potassium	K^+	oxalate	$C_2O_4^{2-}$
rubidium	Rb^+	oxide	O^{2-}
silver	Ag^+	permanganate	MnO_4^-
sodium	Na^+	peroxide	O_2^{2-}
strontium	Sr^{2+}	phosphate	PO_4^{3-}
tin(II)	Sn^{2+}	phosphite	PO_3^{3-}
tin(IV)	Sn^{4+}	phosphide	P^{3-}
zinc	Zn^{2+}	sulfate	SO_4^{2-}
		sulfide	S^{2-}
		sulfite	SO_3^{2-}

◆ The ions combine in a ratio so that the sum of the charges is equal to zero. A method called "crisscross and reduce" will help determine how many of each ion is needed. In this method, the charge of the cation becomes the number of anions present, and the charge of the anion becomes the number of cations present. Na^+ combines with S^{2-} to give Na_2S. Drawing pictures also helps us see the number of each ion required (see Figure 5.1). If the numbers in the "crisscross" end up being numbers that can be factored, such as Pb_2S_2, then the numbers need to be reduced to the lowest possible whole numbers: Pb_2S_2 then becomes PbS.

✓ Sodium sulfide: Na^+ combined with $S^{2-} = Na_2S$. It takes <u>two</u> 1^+ charges to offset <u>one</u> 2^- charge, $(\underline{2} \times 1) + (\underline{1} \times -2) = 0$.

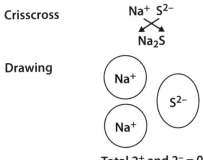

✓ Aluminum oxide: Al^{3+} combined with $O^{2-} = Al_2O_3$. It takes <u>two</u> 3^+ charges to offset <u>three</u> 2^- charges, $(\underline{2} \times 3) + (\underline{3} \times -2) = 0$.

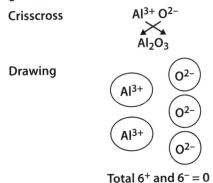

Figure 5.1

◆ Some ions with more than one possible charge will have a Roman numeral in the name to indicate the charge used. For instance, iron(III) is Fe^{3+}.

Some ions are polyatomic, which means that several atoms form a group with a consistent charge, such as the ammonium ion mentioned earlier and the sulfate ion, SO_4^{2-}. If more than one of a polyatomic ion is needed, put the ion in parentheses and the number needed as a subscript after the closing parenthesis (see Figure 5.2).

✓ Aluminum phosphate: Al^{3+} combined with PO_4^{3-} = $AlPO_4$. It takes **one** 3^+ charge to offset **one** 3^- charge, $(\underline{1} \times 3) + (\underline{1} \times -3) = 0$.

$Al_3(PO_4)_3$ and reduce to $AlPO_4$

Total 3^+ and $3^- = 0$

✓ Aluminum sulfate: Al^{3+} combined with SO_4^{2-} = $Al_2(SO_4)_3$. It takes **two** 3^+ charges to offset **three** 2^- charges, $(\underline{2} \times 3) + (\underline{3} \times -2) = 0$.

$Al_2(SO_4)_3$

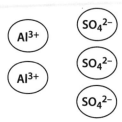

Total 6^+ and $6^- = 0$

✓ Ammonium sulfide: NH_4^+ combined with S^{2-} = $(NH_4)_2S$. It take **two** 1^+ charges to offset **one** 2^- charge, $(\underline{2} \times 1) + (\underline{1} \times -2) = 0$.

NH_4^+ S^{2-}

$(NH_4)_2S$

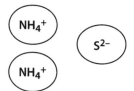

Total 2^+ and $2^- = 0$

Figure 5.2

EXERCISE
5·1

Using the periodic table at the end of this book and Table 5.1 on page 58, write the formula for each of the following compounds.

1. Potassium oxide _____

2. Strontium chloride _____

3. Aluminum nitride _____

4. Lithium phosphide _____

5. Aluminum chlorate _____

6. Beryllium phosphite _____

7. Calcium sulfate _____

8. Sodium nitrate _____

9. Aluminum oxalate _____

10. Ammonium sulfate _____

11. Sodium nitrite _____

12. Potassium nitrate _____

13. Aluminum sulfide _____

14. Iron(II) oxide _____

15. Iron(III) oxide _____

16. Lead(II) acetate _____

17. Gallium chlorate _____

18. Ammonium sulfide _____

19. Silver oxide _____

20. Manganese(IV) oxide _____

Writing the name of an ionic compound from the formula

Writing the name of a compound from the formula is the opposite process of writing the formula from the name. To write the name, consider the following points.

◆ The metal cation name is always written first in the name, and the anion name is written second.
◆ The metal cation is given the name of the metal without changing the ending.
◆ If the metal cation has more than one oxidation state, a Roman numeral is put in parentheses after the name to indicate the state used. To know if this is the case, look on a table with oxidation states given, such as Table 5.1 on page 58. Copper(II) nitrate, for example, indicates that the charge on the copper is 2^+. Most of the metals needing a Roman numeral are transition metals.
◆ The anion has a name ending in *-ide*, *-ate*, or *-ite*. Use Table 5.1 to find which one to use. Usually, single ions end in *-ide* (two exceptions are cyanide, CN^-, and hydroxide, OH^-). Ions containing many atoms, called polyatomic ions, end in *-ate* and *-ite*, such as sulfate, SO_4^{2-}, and sulfite, SO_3^{2-}. If you look closely, you will observe that the number of oxygen atoms in an *-ate* ion is one more than in the corresponding *-ite* ion: sulfate has four oxygen atoms, while sulfite has three. A *per-* in front of an *-ate* ion indicates an additional oxygen atom: chlorate is ClO_3^-, while perchlorate is ClO_4^-. A *hypo-* in front of an *-ite* ion indicates one less oxygen atom: chlorite is ClO_2^-, while hypochlorite, found in bleach, is ClO^-.

Ion name	Number of oxygen atoms
Per___ate	+1
___ate	depends on the ion
___ite	−1
Hypo___ite	−2

Number of atoms in common -*ate* ions			
3		**4**	
Nitrate	NO_3^-	Phosphate	PO_4^{3-}
Carbonate	CO_3^{2-}	Sulfate	SO_4^{2-}
Chlorate	ClO_3^-		
Bromate	BrO_3^-		
Iodate	IO_3^-		

- Even though they are from an old system no longer used by the IUPAC, old names will often be seen on household labels. For instance, Fe^{3+} was called *ferric*. Ferric chloride is now iron(III) chloride, $FeCl_3$. A few examples are listed in the following table:

Ion	Former name	New name
Fe^{3+}	ferric	iron(III)
Fe^{2+}	ferrous	iron(II)
Cu^{2+}	cupric	copper(II)
Cu^+	cuprous	copper(I)
Sn^{4+}	stannic	tin(IV)
Sn^{2+}	stannous	tin(II)

- The first letter of the cation should be capitalized if it starts a sentence; otherwise, the entire name should be lowercase.

Hint: Reversing the crisscross will help identify the charge of the ion.

$Ca(OH)_2$: Ca^{2+} is calcium and OH^- is hydroxide, so the name is calcium hydroxide.

$KMnO_4$: K^+ is potassium and MnO_4^- is permanganate, so the name is potassium permanganate.

$Ni_3(PO_4)_2$: Ni^{2+} is nickel(II) and PO_4^{3-} is phosphate, so the name is nickel(II) phosphate. Always check if a metal ion needs a Roman numeral!

EXERCISE
5·2

Write the names of the following compounds from their formulas.

1. Al_2S_3 _____

2. K_3PO_4 _____

3. $CuSO_4$ _____

4. $Zn(NO_3)_2$ _____

5. $FeCO_3$ _____

6. $Sn(BrO)_2$ _____

7. $PbCl_4$ _____

8. MnO_2 _____

9. $Ca(MnO_4)_2$ _____

10. Cs_2O _____

11. $AgBr$ _____

12. $CrCl_3$ _____

13. K_2CO_3 _____

14. FeS _____

15. $Al(OH)_3$ _____

16. CdS _____

17. $FeCl_3$ _____

18. $Ca_3(PO_4)_2$ _____

19. $Ni(NO_3)_2$ _____

20. PbO _____

Nonmetal-nonmetal combinations

Nonmetal-nonmetal combinations form covalent bonds. Units of these compounds are called molecules and have their own naming system. This system uses the following prefixes:

Number of atoms	Prefix
1	mono-
2	di-
3	tri-
4	tetra-
5	penta-
6	hexa-
7	hepta-
8	octa-
9	nona-
10	deca-

Writing the formula of a covalent compound from the name

Writing the formula of a covalent compound requires remembering the prefixes that are associated with the number of atoms found in the compound. The preceding table can be used as a reference.

- The first word in the name has the name of the first element. If only one atom of the first element is present in the formula, no prefix will be added to the element name.
- The second element in the name will *always* have a prefix to indicate the number of atoms of that element that are in the molecule, and the name will *always* end in *-ide*.

Carbon monoxide: The lack of a prefix on carbon indicates that there is one carbon atom, and the prefix *mono-* indicates that there is one oxygen atom, for a formula of CO.

Dinitrogen trioxide: The prefix *di-* indicates that there are two nitrogen atoms, and the prefix *tri-* indicates that there are three oxygen atoms, for a formula of N_2O_3.

Write the chemical formula for each of the following compounds.

1. Carbon dioxide   _____

2. Sulfur trioxide   _____

3. Dihydrogen monoxide   _____

4. Tetraphosphorus decoxide   _____

5. Disulfur dichloride   _____

6. Silicon tetrafluoride   _____

7. Ditnitrogen tetroxide   _____

8. Nitrogen dioxide   _____

9. Dichlorine heptoxide   _____

10. Carbon disulfide   _____

Writing the name of a covalent compound from the formula

When writing the name of a covalent compound from the formula be sure to follow these pointers.

◆ The first symbol represents the first element in the name. If there is more than one atom of that element in the formula, add the appropriate prefix in front of the element's name.

◆ The second symbol represents the second element (and the second word) in the name. No matter how many atoms are present, add the appropriate prefix and end the name in *-ide*. If the prefix ends in *a*, such as *tetra-*, and the element name begins with a vowel, the *a* can be dropped from the name: tetroxide instead of tetraoxide.

◆ The first letter of the name is capitalized if it starts a sentence; otherwise, the entire name should be lowercase.

> SO_2: Only one sulfur atom is listed, so no prefix is added to *sulfur*; two oxygen atoms are listed, indicating the prefix *di-* for *oxide*. The name is sulfur dioxide.
>
> P_4O_6: Four phosphorus atoms are given, so the prefix *tetra-* is added to *phosphorus*; six oxygen atoms are listed, for a prefix of *hexa-* added to *oxide*. The name is tetraphosphorus hexoxide. Note that the *a* is left on *tetra-* but dropped off *hexa-*.

The exception to this type of naming is when the nonmetal starting the compound is a hydrogen ion and the system is in a water-based solution. See the next section on acids.

Write the name that corresponds to each of the following chemical formulas.

1. N_2O_5 _____

2. CBr_4 _____

3. P_2O_3 _____

4. PCl_3 _____

5. SiO_2 _____

6. BF_3 _____

7. NO _____

8. SF_6 _____

9. ClO_2 _____

10. CO _____

When a hydrogen cation and a nonmetal anion are in solution, this indicates that an acid is present. If the compound is a gas, use the rules for nonmetal-nonmetal combinations found earlier in this chapter. A good practice to use is to first write the name as if it were not an acid, then, if the compound is in aqueous solution (aq), to convert the name to an acid name! An aqueous solution is one where the dissolving medium is water. Acids are a unique form of aqueous solution with a hydrogen cation with the ability to change the pH of a solution.

Some acids have the ability to change the pH more than others. Acids can be classified as strong or weak. Strong acids completely ionize in solution producing hydrogen ions and the anions that in the formula. The most common strong acids include: perchloric, chloric, nitric, sulfuric, hydroiodic, hydrobromic, and hydrochloric. Any other acid is considered weak. Weak acids do not completely ionize in solution. Writing the formulas for these acids will be covered in the next section.

Writing the formula of an acid from the name

When writing the formula of an acid from the name, there are two main types of acids: hydracids and oxoacids. Hydracids contain hydrogen and an anion that does not contain oxygen. Oxoacids contain hydrogen and an anion that does contain oxygen.

- ♦ If the name begins with *hydro-*, hydrogen has combined with an anion ending in *-ide*: *hydrochloric* indicates that H^+ has combined with chloride, Cl^-. To determine how many of each atom is present, the sum of the charges must add up to zero. In this case, $1 + -1 = 0$, so the formula is HCl. Again, the crisscross method can be used to determine the formula. Note that HCl can exist as a pure gas, when its name is hydrogen chloride—but in aqueous solution it is named hydrochloric acid. If this seems confusing, it is! You will have to try to remember the distinction. The same applies to HCN (hydrogen cyanide gas, or hydrocyanic acid).

◆ If the name of the acid does not begin with *hydro-*, H^+ is still present in the formula. This is an indication that the anion used ends in either *-ate* or *-ite*. To know which was used, look at the ending of the acid name; if it ends in *-ic*, the anion used ends in *-ate*, and if it ends in *-ous*, the anion used ends in *-ite*. Again, to determine how many of each part is present, the sum of the charges must equal zero. For instance, the *-ic* ending in *sulfuric acid* indicates that H^+ was combined with sulfate, SO_4^{2-}. It takes two 1^+ charges to offset the one 2^- charge of sulfate, resulting in a formula of H_2SO_4.

Ending of anion name	Indication of H^+ in acid name	Ending of acid name
-ide	Hydro-	-ic
-ate		-ic
-ite		-ous

Hydrofluoric acid: The prefix *hydro-* indicates that H^+ has combined with fluoride, F^-. $(1 \times 1) + (1 \times -1) = 0$, so the formula is HF.

Phosphoric acid: The ending *-ic* indicates that H^+ has combined with phosphate, PO_4^{3-}. $(3 \times 1) + (1 \times -3) = 0$, resulting in a formula of H_3PO_4.

Chlorous acid: The ending *-ous* indicates that H^+ has combined with chlorite, ClO_2^-. $(1 \times 1) + (1 \times -1) = 0$, resulting in the formula $HClO_2$.

EXERCISE 5·5

Write the formula of each acid listed below.

1. Bromic acid _____

2. Periodic acid _____

3. Hydroiodic acid _____

4. Hydrofluoric acid _____

5. Permanganic acid _____

6. Sulfurous acid _____

7. Carbonic acid _____

8. Nitric acid _____

9. Acetic acid _____

10. Phosphoric acid _____

Writing the name of an acid from the formula

Writing the name of an acid from the formula is the opposite of writing the formula from the name. Use the following information to help you acquire this skill.

◆ The acid formula begins with H, but whether or not the name begins with *hydrogen* depends on what has been combined with the H^+.

- If the name of the anion present ends in *-ide*, the acid name begins with the prefix *hydro-* in front of the anion's root name, and the ending of the anion's name changes to *-ic*. For HCN, the anion present is CN^-, which is cyanide. The *-ide* suffix changes to *-ic* and the prefix *hydro-* is placed in front of the root *cyan*: we write *hydrocyanic acid.*
- If the name of the anion present ends in *-ate*, only the ending of the anion's name changes, to *-ic*. $HClO_4$ has the anion ClO_4^-, which is perchlorate. The *-ate* tells us to write *perchloric acid.*
- If the name of the anion present ends in *-ite*, only the ending of the anion's name changes, to *-ous*. HClO has the anion ClO^-, which is hypochlorite. The *-ite* tells us to write the name as *hypochlorous acid.*

> HBr: Br^- is bromide, so the name is hydrobromic acid.
>
> HNO_3: NO_3^- is nitrate, so the name is nitric acid.
>
> HNO_2: NO_2^- is nitrite, so the name is nitrous acid.

EXERCISE
5·6

Write the name of each of the following acids.

1. HI _____

2. H_3PO_4 _____

3. H_2CO_3 _____

4. HFO_2 _____

5. $HBrO_2$ _____

6. HCl _____

7. $H_2C_2O_4$ _____

8. HF _____

9. HNO_2 _____

10. H_2SO_3 _____

Introduction to organic compounds

Organic compounds are molecules made of carbon(s) and saturated with hydrogen. This is only an introduction to organic naming; organic chemistry is its own branch of chemistry. We will look only at *alkanes*, in which the number of hydrogen atoms compared to the number of carbon atoms always follows the formula C_nH_{2n+2}, where *n* is the number of carbon atoms in the formula. In the compounds that follow this general formula, the carbons link together to form continuous unbranched chains or branched chains.

Writing the formula of an unbranched alkane from the name

Writing the formula of an organic compound follows a different set of steps and prefixes.

- The number of carbons in the chain is indicated by a prefix. Some of these prefixes are different from those used earlier in the naming of covalent compounds.

Number of carbon atoms	Prefix
1	meth-
2	eth-
3	prop-
4	but-
5	pent-
6	hex-
7	hept-
8	oct-
9	non-
10	dec-

- The *-ane* ending tells us to use the formula $H = 2n + 2$ to determine the number of hydrogen atoms in the formula, where n is the number of carbon atoms.

Methane: *meth-* indicates one carbon atom, so the number of hydrogen atoms is $2(1) + 2 = 4$. The formula is CH_4.

Butane: *but-* means four carbon atoms, so the number of hydrogen atoms is $2(4) + 2 = 10$. The formula is C_4H_{10}.

EXERCISE
5·7

Write the formula for each of the following unbranched alkanes.

1. Propane _____

2. Octane _____

3. Pentane _____

4. Decane _____

5. Nonane _____

6. Hexane _____

7. Heptane _____

8. Methane _____

9. Ethane _____

10. Butane _____

Writing the name of an unbranched alkane from the formula

To write the name of an unbranched alkane from the formula, follow these steps.

- Look at the number of carbons in the formula and use the organic prefix representing that number.
- If the number of hydrogen atoms is equal to $2n + 2$, the name ends in *-ane*.

C_2H_6: Two carbon atoms indicate that the prefix used is *eth-*, and six hydrogen atoms are equal to $2n + 2$, so the name is ethane.

C_3H_8: Three carbon atoms indicate that the prefix used is *prop-*, and eight hydrogen atoms are equal to $2n + 2$, so the name is propane.

EXERCISE 5·8

For each of the following alkane formulas, write the name of the molecule.

1. C_9H_{20} _____

2. C_6H_{14} _____

3. C_7H_{16} _____

4. C_5H_{10} _____

5. CH_4 _____

6. C_2H_6 _____

7. C_3H_8 _____

8. C_4H_{10} _____

9. C_8H_{18} _____

10. $C_{10}H_{22}$ _____

Many other organic compounds exist, but naming these could be an entire book in itself! Figure 5.3 may help you determine which naming system to use.

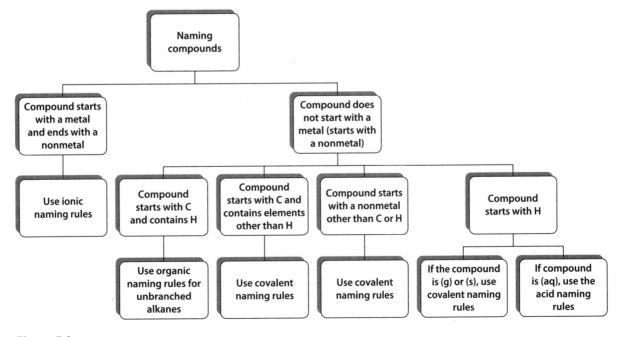

Figure 5.3

EXERCISE
5·9

Look at the formula provided and determine whether the substance listed should be named as an acid (A), a metal-nonmetal combination (M-NM), a nonmetal-nonmetal combination (NM-NM), a molecular compound (M), or none of the choices given (N).

1. K_3PO_4 __________
2. $AuBr_3$ __________
3. CS_2 __________
4. $MgCO_3$ __________
5. HCl(g) __________
6. HI(aq) __________
7. NO_2 __________
8. KF __________
9. $Al(ClO)_3$ __________
10. H_2SO_4(aq) __________
11. CuBr __________
12. $AgNO_2$ __________
13. P_2O_5 __________
14. $(NH_4)_2C_2O_4$ __________
15. NaBr __________

Match the formula in the first column to the name in the second column. If there is no matching name for a formula, determine the correct name.

1. K_3PO_4 _____   A. Hydrochloric acid

2. $AuBr_3$ _____   B. Ammonium oxalate

3. CS_2 _____   C. Aluminum chlorate

4. $MgCO_3$ _____   D. Phosphorus monofluoride

5. $HCl(g)$ _____   E. Silver nitrite

6. $HI(aq)$ _____   F. Diphosphorus pentoxide

7. NO_2 _____   G. Potassium monofluoride

8. KF _____   H. Nitrogen dioxide

9. $Al(ClO)_3$ _____   I. Gold(III) bromide

10. $H_2SO_4(aq)$ _____   J. Hydrogen iodide

11. $CuBr$ _____   K. Magnesium carbonate

12. $AgNO_2$ _____   L. Potassium phosphate

13. P_2O_5 _____   M. Hydrogen chloride

14. $(NH_4)_2C_2O_4$ _____   N. Copper(I) bromide

15. $NaBr$ _____   O. None of the choices match

Match the name in the first column to the correct formula in the second column.

1. Butane _____   A. CH_4

2. Decane _____   B. C_2H_6

3. Ethane _____   C. C_3H_8

4. Heptane _____   D. C_4H_{10}

5. Hexane _____   E. C_5H_{12}

6. Methane _____   F. C_6H_{14}

7. Nonane _____   G. C_7H_{16}

8. Octane _____   H. C_8H_{18}

9. Pentane _____   I. C_9H_{20}

10. Propane _____   J. $C_{10}H_{22}$

Chemical reactions

When elements or compounds are placed together with other elements or compounds, they may or may not react with one another. Most reactions require the addition of energy to break the existing bonds in the reactants so new bonds can be made to form products. This added energy is called the *activation energy*. Besides having the right energy, the species reacting together must also collide with one another in the proper orientation to react. During a reaction there may be several collisions that occur that cause intermediate species to form. The accounting for these intermediate species is called the *reaction mechanism*. Even if two substances known to react are put together, a reaction may not occur.

When the substances do react, we write an equation to represent what occurs. An equation is an accounting of the atoms involved in the reaction. Since atoms are not created or destroyed in regular reactions (only nuclear ones can do that), the number of atoms on each side of the equation must remain the same—in other words, the equation must be balanced. This is called conservation of atoms (or conservation of mass). The *reactants* are what you start with and are found on the left side of the equation. After the reactants, an arrow with its head pointed toward the right is written. The *products* are what are formed in the reaction and are found on the right side of this arrow. The arrow can be read as "to form" or "yields," but in mathematical terms it is an equation, since all atoms listed on the left must equal those on the right. Note that it is always the *arrangement* of the atoms that changes in a chemical reaction, *not* the total number. There are a few basic steps to follow when writing chemical-reaction equations.

Writing and balancing chemical equations

First, write all the formulas for the elements and compounds involved, using the rules previously learned in Chapter 5. Once these are written, keep in mind *the formula cannot change*. Note it is imperative to know the *symbols* for the atoms of each element. The resulting equation with all the formulas in place is called a *skeleton equation*.

Second, count the number of each atom on each side of the equation. If they are not the same, add coefficients in front of the formulas to balance.

What are coefficients? They are numbers you put *in front* of a compound or element to say how many are needed, just like in a cooking recipe: 2 cups of flour. The coefficient is the amount and the formula is the compound. In the flour example, where the flour is the compound, the coefficient is the 2. In a chemical reaction, when you need two sodium chloride formula units you write 2NaCl. Drawing a picture with each type of atom represented can help make sure all atoms are accounted for on each side of the equation.

Sample Problem 1:   Sodium phosphate solution is added to a solution of silver nitrate, forming a solution of sodium nitrate and a precipitate of silver phosphate.

First, write all the formulas:

Sodium is Na^+ and phosphate is PO_4^{3-}, making sodium phosphate $Na_3PO_4(aq)$.

Silver is Ag^+ and nitrate is NO_3^-, making silver nitrate $AgNO_3(aq)$.

Sodium is Na^+ and nitrate is NO_3^-, making sodium nitrate $NaNO_3(aq)$.

Silver is Ag^+ and phosphate is PO_4^{3-}, making silver phosphate $Ag_3PO_4(s)$.

Next, write all the formulas in an equation and balance the number of each atom on each side of the equation. The skeleton equation without coefficients is given in Figure 6.1.

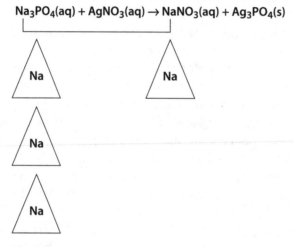

Figure 6.1

There are three sodium atoms on the left and only one sodium atom on the right. Adding a coefficient of 3 to the sodium nitrate on the right side of the equation balances the sodium atoms.

$$Na_3PO_4(aq) + AgNO_3(aq) \rightarrow 3NaNO_3(aq) + Ag_3PO_4(s)$$

The formula of a compound cannot change, only the number of units present.

Looking at the phosphorus atoms (see Figure 6.2), there is one on each side, so no additional coefficient is needed.

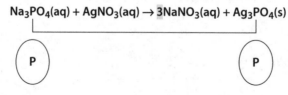

Figure 6.2

Next, look at the silver atoms (in Figure 6.3).

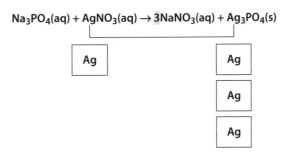

$$Na_3PO_4(aq) + AgNO_3(aq) \rightarrow 3NaNO_3(aq) + Ag_3PO_4(s)$$

Figure 6.3

There is one on the left and three on the right. Adding a 3 in front of the silver nitrate gives

$$Na_3PO_4(aq) + \mathbf{3}AgNO_3(aq) \rightarrow 3NaNO_3(aq) + Ag_3PO_4(s).$$

Checking the nitrogen atoms, there are now three on the left and three on the right, since the coefficients distribute to *all* the atoms that follow in the formula (see Figure 6.4).

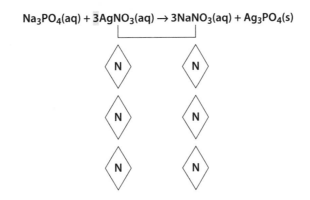

$$Na_3PO_4(aq) + \mathbf{3}AgNO_3(aq) \rightarrow 3NaNO_3(aq) + Ag_3PO_4(s)$$

Figure 6.4

Now, checking the oxygen atoms in Figure 6.5, there are 13 on each side!

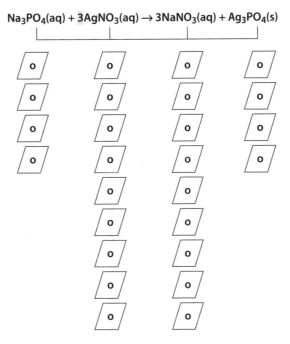

$$Na_3PO_4(aq) + \mathbf{3}AgNO_3(aq) \rightarrow 3NaNO_3(aq) + Ag_3PO_4(s)$$

Figure 6.5

This may seem really long, but most equations balance very quickly once you have the formulas written correctly *and* you have worked many practice examples. One tip is to imagine you are building model buildings with a model set such as Legos. You take apart one building and build a different one, but you want to use up *all* the blocks, with none left over.

Sample Problem 2:   Lead(II) nitrate solution is mixed with a solution of potassium iodide to form a precipitate of lead(II) iodide and a solution of potassium nitrate.

First, balance all compounds in the equation. See Chapter 5 if you need to review this.

Lead(II) nitrate: Pb^{2+} combined with NO_3^- is $Pb(NO_3)_2$(aq).

Potassium iodide: K^+ combined with I^- is KI(aq).

Lead(II) iodide: Pb^{2+} combined with I^- is PbI_2(s).

Potassium nitrate: K^+ combined with NO_3^- is KNO_3(aq).

Next, write the skeleton equation with all the compounds in it:

$$Pb(NO_3)_2(aq) + KI(aq) \rightarrow PbI_2(s) + KNO_3(aq)$$

Balance each atom to determine if a coefficient is needed.

Pb—1:1, no coefficient needed.

N—2:1, so add a coefficient of 2 to the product side: $2KNO_3$.

O—6:6, using the coefficient of 2 that was just added.

K—1:2, so a coefficient of 2 needs to be added to the reactant, making $2KI$.

I—2:2.

Now, write the fully balanced equation:

$$Pb(NO_3)_2(aq) + 2KI(aq) \rightarrow PbI_2(s) + 2KNO_3(aq)$$

Sample Problem 3:   Zinc metal is added to a solution of copper(II) sulfate to form a solution of zinc sulfate and copper metal.

First, balance all compounds in the equation.

Zinc: Zn(s).

Copper(II) sulfate: Cu^{2+} combined with SO_4^{2-} is $CuSO_4$(aq).

Zinc sulfate: Zn^{2+} combined with SO_4^{2-} is $ZnSO_4$(aq).

Copper: Cu(s).

Next, write the skeleton equation with all the compounds in it:

$$Zn(s) + CuSO_4(aq) \rightarrow ZnSO_4(aq) + Cu(s)$$

Next, balance each atom to determine if a coefficient is needed.

Zn—1:1, no coefficient needed.

Cu—1:1, no coefficient needed.

S—1:1, no coefficient needed.

O—4:4, no coefficient needed.

Now write the fully balanced equation:

$$Zn(s) + CuSO_4(aq) \rightarrow ZnSO_4(aq) + Cu(s)$$

Write skeleton and balanced equations for each of the following chemical reactions.

1. Solutions of barium chloride and sodium carbonate react to form aqueous sodium chloride and a precipitate of barium carbonate.

   _____

   _____

2. Solutions of potassium hydroxide and iron(III) chloride are mixed and iron(III) hydroxide precipitates in a solution of potassium chloride.

   _____

   _____

3. Copper wire is placed in a solution of silver nitrate, and metallic silver forms in a solution of copper(II) nitrate.

   _____

   _____

4. Chlorine gas is bubbled into a solution of potassium bromide, forming bromine liquid and potassium chloride solution.

   _____

   _____

5. Solutions of barium chloride and zinc sulfate are mixed to form a solution of zinc chloride and a precipitate of barium sulfate.

   _____

   _____

6. Solutions of aluminum nitrate and sodium hydroxide are mixed to form a solution of sodium nitrate and a precipitate of aluminum hydroxide.

   _____

   _____

7. Aluminum metal is placed in a solution of copper(II) chloride, and a solution of aluminum chloride forms along with copper metal.

   _____

   _____

8. Solutions of barium chloride and sodium sulfate are mixed to form a solution of sodium chloride and a precipitate of barium sulfate.

   _____

   _____

9. Sulfur trioxide gas is heated and decomposes to sulfur dioxide gas and oxygen gas.

_____

_____

10. Chlorine gas is bubbled into a solution of lithium iodide to form lithium chloride solution and iodine solid.

_____

_____

Combination, or synthesis

There are several basic types of reactions. *Combination*, or *synthesis*, occurs when two or more species combine and make one product. These are easy to recognize, since only one product is formed. If two elements are combined, the only possible reaction is combination. The general format appears as $A + B \rightarrow AB$. There are a few rules that will help with predictions.

◆ Metal oxides combining with carbon dioxide yield metal carbonates, e.g., solid calcium oxide reacts with carbon dioxide gas to form solid calcium carbonate.

$$CaO(s) + CO_2(g) \rightarrow CaCO_3(s)$$

◆ An element plus an element yields a compound. The element listed first in the compound will be the one forming a positive charge. If oxygen is one of the elements, it is always last; if hydrogen is one of the elements, it is usually first. Hydrogen gas reacts with oxygen gas to form liquid water.

$$2H_2(g) + O_2(g) \rightarrow 2H_2O(l)$$

Solid magnesium ribbon, when ignited, will burn with oxygen in the air to form solid magnesium oxide.

$$Mg(s) + O_2(g) \rightarrow 2MgO(s)$$

◆ Nonmetal oxides plus water yield an acid, e.g., carbon dioxide combined with water yields carbonic acid.

$$CO_2(g) + H_2O(l) \rightarrow H_2CO_3(aq)$$

EXERCISE
6·2

Predict the product of each of the following reactions and write a balanced equation for the reaction.

1. Iron filings react with oxygen in the air. Hint: the iron(III) compound is formed.

_____

2. When magnesium metal is ignited in nitrogen gas.

_____

3. Sulfur trioxide gas reacts with water droplets in the air to form an acid.

_____

4. Calcium metal reacts with oxygen in the air.

_____

5. Hydrogen gas reacts with chlorine gas.

_____

6. Sodium metal reacts with chlorine gas.

_____

7. Sodium oxide solid reacts with water.

_____

8. Silver metal reacts with oxygen in the air.

_____

9. Dinitrogen trioxide reacts with water vapor in the air.

_____

10. Aluminum metal reacts with oxygen in the air.

_____

Decomposition

The reverse of combination, *decomposition* starts with one reactant that breaks apart, often because the substance is heated. Look for one reactant before the arrow. The general format appears as $AB \rightarrow A + B$. A decomposition reaction is often the reverse of a synthesis reaction. For example, if carbon dioxide and water combine to make carbonic acid in a synthesis reaction, when carbonic acid decomposes it forms water and carbon dioxide.

♦ Metal carbonates decompose to metal oxides and carbon dioxide; e.g., solid magnesium carbonate decomposes when heated to solid magnesium oxide and carbon dioxide.

$$MgCO_3(s) \rightarrow MgO(s) + CO_2(g)$$

Solid sodium carbonate decomposes when heated into solid sodium oxide and carbon dioxide gas.

$$Na_2CO_3(s) \rightarrow Na_2O(s) + CO_2(g)$$

♦ A compound of two elements breaks into the two elements; e.g., solid magnesium nitride decomposes upon heating into magnesium metal and nitrogen gas.

$$Mg_3N_2(s) \rightarrow 3Mg(s) + N_2(g)$$

♦ Acids decompose into water and a nonmetal oxide; e.g., aqueous sulfuric acid decomposes into liquid water and sulfur trioxide gas.

$$H_2SO_4(aq) \rightarrow H_2O(l) + SO_3(g)$$

♦ Metal chlorates decompose into metal chlorides and oxygen gas; e.g., solid potassium chlorate decomposes into solid potassium chloride and oxygen gas.

$$2KClO_3(s) \rightarrow 2KCl(s) + 3O_2(g)$$

♦ Hydrogen peroxide decomposes into water and oxygen gas; e.g., liquid hydrogen peroxide decomposes to oxygen gas and liquid water.

$$2H_2O_2(l) \rightarrow O_2(g) + 2H_2O(l)$$

♦ Bases decompose to form a metallic oxide and liquid water; e.g., upon heating gently, solid magnesium hydroxide decomposes into solid magnesium oxide and water vapor.

$$Mg(OH)_2(s) \rightarrow MgO(s) + H_2O(l)$$

EXERCISE
6·3

Predict the products of each of the following reactions and write a balanced equation for what occurs.

1. Liquid water decomposes when an electrical current is added.

_____

2. When heated, solid potassium chlorate releases a gas and leaves a new solid salt behind.

_____

3. Solid mercury(II) oxide decomposes when heated.

_____

4. Carbonic acid solution decomposes upon heating.

_____

5. Calcium hydroxide solution decomposes upon heating.

_____

6. Lithium carbonate solid decomposes upon heating.

_____

7. When heated, solid sodium chlorate decomposes.

_____

8. Liquid sodium chloride is decomposed by electrolysis.

_____

9. When heated, solid silver oxide decomposes.

_____

10. When heated gently, aqueous sulfurous acid decomposes.

_____

Single replacement

When an element combines with a compound to form a different element and a new compound, a single element is replaced on the product side. Hence, it is called *single replacement* or sometimes single displacement. The general format appears as $A + BC \rightarrow AC + B$ or $A + BC \rightarrow BA + C$. In the first example here, the reactant metallic element replaces a metal in the compound, and in the second example, the reactant nonmetallic element replaces the nonmetal in the compound.

Example 1: A solid sodium pellet is placed in a solution of copper(II) nitrate and reacts to form a solution of sodium nitrate and solid copper.

$$2Na(s) + Cu(NO_3)_2(aq) \rightarrow 2NaNO_3(aq) + Cu(s)$$

Example 2: Chlorine gas is bubbled into a solution of sodium bromide to form a solution of sodium chloride and liquid bromine.

$$Cl_2(g) + 2NaBr(aq) \rightarrow 2NaCl(aq) + Br_2(l)$$

Not every metal can replace another metal. Metals have a reactivity order (see Figure 6.6), where a metal can only replace a metal ion below it in the reactivity series. This means lithium can replace any metal ion in solution.

Li
K
Ba
Ca
Na
Mg
Al
Zn
Cr
Fe
Cd
Co
Ni
Sn
Pb
H_2
Cu
Ag
Hg
Pt
Au

Figure 6.6

On the other end of the series, gold cannot replace any other metal ion in solution.

Halogens also have a reactivity series (see Figure 6.7) and can similarly only replace ones that are below them in the series. Fluorine can replace all other halide ions in solution, while iodine, at the bottom, cannot replace any others.

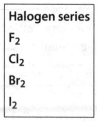

Halogen series

F_2

Cl_2

Br_2

I_2

Figure 6.7

Many metals are capable of replacing hydrogen in acids, some can replace hydrogen in steam (very hot water), and some metals can even replace hydrogen in cold water. When you look carefully at the metals, you will observe fewer choices each time but they are the same metals! Those that can do all three are bolded.

◆ Metals replacing hydrogen in acids are **Li**, **K**, **Ba**, **Ca**, **Na**, Mg, Al, Zn, Cr, Fe, Cd, Co, Ni, Sn, and Pb. Look carefully again at the metal reactivity series in Figure 6.6 on the previous page. Do you notice a trend?

Example 1: A solid zinc pellet is placed in a solution of hydrochloric acid to form a solution of zinc chloride and hydrogen gas.

$$Zn(s) + 2HCl(aq) \rightarrow ZnCl_2(aq) + H_2(g)$$

Example 2: Aluminum foil is placed in a solution of hydrochloric acid to form a solution of aluminum chloride and hydrogen gas.

$$2Al(s) + 6HCl(aq) \rightarrow 2AlCl_3(aq) + 3H_2(g)$$

◆ Metals replacing hydrogen in steam are **Li**, **K**, **Ba**, **Ca**, **Na**, Mg, Al, Zn, Cr, Fe, and Cd. Again, look at Figure 6.6 to see the trend.

Example 1: Solid iron is placed in steam to form an iron(II) hydroxide solution and hydrogen gas.

$$Fe(s) + 2H_2O(l) \rightarrow Fe(OH)_2(aq) + H_2(g)$$

Example 2: Magnesium ribbon is placed in steam, reacting to form a magnesium hydroxide solution and hydrogen gas.

$$Mg(s) + 2H_2O(l) \rightarrow Mg(OH)_2(aq) + H_2(g)$$

◆ Metals replacing hydrogen in cold water are **Li**, **K**, **Ba**, **Ca**, and **Na**.

Example 1: Solid sodium is placed in cold water to form a solution of sodium hydroxide and hydrogen gas.

$$2Na(s) + 2H_2O(l) \rightarrow 2NaOH(aq) + H_2(g)$$

Example 2: Solid calcium is placed in water to form a solution of calcium hydroxide and hydrogen gas.

$$Ca(s) + 2H_2O(l) \rightarrow Ca(OH)_2(aq) + H_2(g)$$

Predict the products of each of the following reactions and write a balanced equation for what occurs.

1. A piece of lithium metal is added to cold water.

_____

2. Fluorine gas is added to a solution of potassium iodide.

_____

3. A zinc bar is placed in steam.

_____

4. Sulfuric acid is added to a sheet of lead metal.

_____

5. Zinc pellets are placed in a solution of hydrochloric acid.

_____

6. Chlorine gas is bubbled into a solution of potassium bromide.

_____

7. Potassium metal is added to water.

_____

8. Copper wire is added to a solution of silver nitrate. Hint: one of the products contains copper(II).

_____

9. Fluorine gas is bubbled into a solution of sodium chloride.

_____

10. Iron filings are added to a solution of copper(II) nitrate. Hint: one of the products contains iron(II).

_____

Double replacement

When two compounds combine and form two new compounds by switching anions, it is called *double replacement* or double displacement. There are several types of double displacement reactions. One type are reactions that form precipitates. This type of reaction often occurs in solution (two dissolved substances), and one or both products formed are a solid called a *precipitate*. There are rules to determine which ones form precipitates. Right now, let's just look at the format: the general format is $AB + CD \rightarrow AD + CB$.

Example 1: Solutions of silver nitrate and sodium chloride are mixed to form a precipitate of silver chloride and a solution of sodium nitrate.

$$AgNO_3(aq) + NaCl(aq) \rightarrow AgCl(s) + NaNO_3(aq)$$

Example 2: Solutions of zinc sulfate and barium nitrate are mixed.

$$ZnSO_4(aq) + Ba(NO_3)_2(aq) \rightarrow Zn(NO_3)_2(aq) + BaSO_4(s)$$

How does one tell if a precipitate forms? Solubility rules are used, but rather than have you derive these rules from experiments or memorize them, Table 6.1 will be used as a reference. Use the first column to locate the cation and then move your finger across until the column with the desired anion is reached. At the intersection of the cation and anion, S indicates solubility, which means the compound stays in solution (think $S = stays$ solution); and I indicates insolubility, so the compound is forming a precipitate (think $I = in$ precipitate)—but is noted as a solid, (s), in the balanced equation. This can be very confusing. The S on the solubility table does not mean a solid is formed. Solubility tables differ in format, but all are based on the same principles.

Table 6.1 Solubility Table of Selected Ions in Aqueous Solutions

	Br^-	Cl^-	ClO_3^-	I^-	NO_3^-	OH^-	PO_4^{3-}	SO_4^{2-}
Ag^+	I	I	S	I	S	I	I	I
Al^{3+}	S	S	S	S	S	I	I	S
Ba^{2+}	S	S	S	S	S	S	I	I
Ca^{2+}	S	S	S	S	S	I	I	I
Cu^{2+}	S	S	S	S	S	I	I	S
Hg^{2+}	I	I	S	I	S	I	I	I
K^+	S	S	S	S	S	S	S	S
Li^+	S	S	S	S	S	S	S	S
Mg^{2+}	S	S	S	S	S	I	I	S
Na^+	S	S	S	S	S	S	S	S
Ni^{2+}	S	S	S	S	S	I	I	S
Pb^{2+}	I	I	S	I	S	I	I	I
Sr^{2+}	S	S	S	S	S	I	I	I
Zn^{2+}	S	S	S	S	S	I	I	S

EXERCISE
6·5

Predict the products of each of the following reactions and write a balanced equation for what occurs.

1. Solutions of ammonium iodide and silver nitrate react.

2. A sodium sulfate solution is mixed with a solution of lead(II) nitrate.

3. A solution of copper(II) chloride is added to a potassium hydroxide solution.

4. Solutions of aluminum nitrate and sodium phosphate react.

_____

5. Solutions of sodium chloride and lead(II) nitrate react.

_____

6. Solutions of potassium hydroxide and nickel(II) nitrate react.

_____

7. Solutions of barium chlorate and potassium sulfate are mixed.

_____

8. Lithium hydroxide solution is added to a solution of magnesium chloride.

_____

9. Strontium bromide solution is added to a solution of nickel(II) sulfate.

_____

10. Zinc iodide solution is added to a solution of potassium hydroxide.

_____

Combustion

Combustion reactions occur when hydrocarbons burn in the presence of oxygen gas. It will be assumed all combustion reactions are complete, meaning the only products formed are carbon dioxide and water. During incomplete combustion, such as the burning of a candle, carbon monoxide and carbon soot also form.

Example 1: Propane burns in air to form carbon dioxide and water vapor.

$$C_3H_8(g) + 5O_2(g) \rightarrow 3CO_2(g) + 4H_2O(g)$$

Example 2: Methane burns in air to form carbon dioxide and water vapor.

$$CH_4(g) + 2O_2(g) \rightarrow CO_2(g) + 2H_2O(g)$$

EXERCISE
6·6

Write a balanced equation for each of the following complete combustion reactions.

1. Butane gas burns in air.

_____

2. Heptane gas burns in air.

_____

3. Decane gas burns in air.

_____

4. Octane gas burns in air.

_____

5. Ethane gas burns in air.

_____

Acid-base

Acid-base reactions are a unique form of double displacement reactions that generally occur without a precipitate forming. The acids and bases react as a hydrogen ion is transferred from the acid to the base, making a new product. There are different definitions of acids, but the most commonly used definition of an acid is a proton donor. Remember, an H$^+$ (hydrogen ion) is only a proton. More about acid-base reactions is included in Chapter 10.

Example 1: Solutions of hydrochloric acid and sodium hydroxide are mixed to form water and a solution of sodium chloride.

$$HCl(aq) + NaOH(aq) \rightarrow H_2O(l) + NaCl(aq)$$

Example 2: Solutions of hydrobromic acid and barium hydroxide are mixed to form a solution of barium bromide and water.

$$2HBr(aq) + Ba(OH)_2(aq) \rightarrow 2H_2O(l) + BaBr_2(aq).$$

Example 3: Some products when formed are unstable and will subsequently decompose into other products. For example, the weak acid carbonic acid decomposes to form carbon dioxide gas and liquid water.

$$H_2CO_3(aq) \rightarrow CO_2(g) + H_2O(l)$$

Example 4: Another example would be ammonium hydroxide, which decomposes to form ammonia gas and liquid water.

$$NH_4OH(aq) \rightarrow NH_3(g) + H_2O(l)$$

EXERCISE
6·7

Predict the products of each of the following reactions and write a balanced equation for what occurs. Assume the reactions have sufficient reactant to fully react.

1. Solid nickel(III) hydroxide is added to a solution of hydroiodic acid.

_____

2. Solutions of sulfuric acid and potassium hydroxide are mixed.

_____

3. A solution of calcium hydroxide is added to a solution of nitric acid.

_____

4. Solutions of sulfuric acid and sodium hydroxide are mixed.

_____

5. Solutions of hydrofluoric acid and potassium hydroxide are mixed.

_____

6. Solutions of phosphoric acid and lithium hydroxide are mixed.

_____

7. Solutions of calcium hydroxide and hydrochloric acid are mixed.

_____

8. Magnesium hydroxide solution and phosphoric acid solution are mixed.

_____

9. Barium carbonate solid is stirred into hydrochloric acid solution.

_____

10. Sulfuric acid solution is added to a solution of lithium hydroxide.

_____

Ionic and net ionic equations

An equation indicates the reactants and products in the overall reaction but is not an indication of the steps of the reaction or the factors driving the reaction to occur. To help understand this, there are other forms of equation writing. An ionic equation goes one additional step and, for water-based solutions, indicates in the equation if ions are formed. Depending on the solution, the species formed may be ionized. Ionizing species include strong acids, strong bases, and ionic compounds that dissolve in water. Refer back to Table 6.1 on page 84 to determine if a specific ionic compound is soluble. Non-ionizing species include weak acids, weak bases, and molecular compounds. These species are not separated in ionic equations. All water-based solutions are designated with *(aq)* behind them in the equation. So this reaction notation differs from a balanced equation, since it shows the actual species that are present in the solution. Note that some species—those that are liquids, solids, or gases—remain the same.

$$Zn(s) + 2HCl(aq) \rightarrow ZnCl_2(aq) + H_2(g)$$

would be changed to

$$Zn(s) + 2H^+(aq) + 2Cl^-(aq) \rightarrow Zn^{2+}(aq) + 2Cl^-(aq) + H_2(g).$$

In the last equation, $2Cl^-$ exist on both sides of the equation. These are called *spectator ions* and were not actually involved in the reaction. In a net ionic equation, the spectators are cancelled out. This is important, as the net equation then shows the actual reaction driving the overall equation.

$$Zn(s) + 2H^+(aq) + 2Cl^-(aq) \rightarrow Zn^{2+}(aq) + 2Cl^-(aq) + H_2(g)$$

would thus be changed to

$$Zn(s) + 2H^+(aq) \rightarrow Zn^{2+}(aq) + H_2(g).$$

For the reaction $ZnSO_4(aq) + Ba(NO_3)_2(aq) \rightarrow Zn(NO_3)_2(aq) + BaSO_4(s)$, the ionic equation would be

$$Zn^{2+}(aq) + SO_4^{2-}(aq) + Ba^{2+}(aq) + 2NO_3^-(aq) \rightarrow Zn^{2+}(aq) + 2NO_3^-(aq) + BaSO_4(s)$$

and the net ionic equation would be

$$SO_4^{2-}(aq) + Ba^{2+}(aq) \rightarrow BaSO_4(s)$$

after the spectator ions of $Zn^{2+}(aq)$ and $2NO_3^-(aq)$ were cancelled.

For the reaction $HCl(aq) + NaOH(aq) \rightarrow H_2O(l) + NaCl(aq)$, the ionic equation would be

$$H^+(aq) + Cl^-(aq) + Na^+(aq) + OH^-(aq) \rightarrow H_2O(l) + Na^+(aq) + Cl^-(aq)$$

and the net ionic equation would be

$$H^+(aq) + OH^-(aq) \rightarrow H_2O(l).$$

EXERCISE

6·8

For each of the following, write a balanced equation, a balanced ionic equation, and a balanced net ionic equation.

1. Solutions of sodium phosphate and silver nitrate react.

_____

_____

_____

2. A solution of potassium hydroxide is added to a solution of strontium chloride.

_____

_____

_____

3. Bromine liquid is added to a solution of potassium iodide.

_____

_____

_____

4. Solutions of hydrochloric acid and potassium hydroxide are mixed.

_____

_____

_____

5. Solutions of sodium sulfide and silver chlorate are mixed.

_____

_____

_____

6. Chlorine gas is bubbled into a solution of lithium bromide.

_____

_____

_____

7. Solutions of ammonium phosphate and barium hydroxide are mixed.

_____

_____

_____

8. Copper wire is placed in a solution of silver nitrate.

_____

_____

_____

9. Solutions of calcium hydroxide and sulfuric acid are mixed.

_____

_____

_____

_____

EXERCISE
6·9

Identify the type of each of the following reactions, using S for synthesis or combination, D for decomposition, SD for single displacement, DD for double displacement, and C for combustion.

1. $H_3PO_4(aq) + 3NaOH(aq) \rightarrow Na_3PO_4(aq) + 3H_2O(l)$ _____

2. $4Al(s) + 3O_2(g) \rightarrow 2Al_2O_3(s)$ _____

3. $CuCO_3(s) \rightarrow CuO(s) + CO_2(g)$ _____

4. $2C_2H_6(g) + 7O_2(g) \rightarrow 4CO_2(g) + 6H_2O(g)$ _____

5. $Mg(s) + 2HCl(aq) \rightarrow MgCl_2(aq) + H_2(g)$ _____

EXERCISE
6·10

Predict the products of each of the following reactions and write a balanced equation for what occurs.

1. A piece of cadmium metal reacts with hydrochloric acid.

_____

2. Pentane gas undergoes complete combustion in air.

_____

3. Nitrogen gas reacts with hydrogen gas.

_____

4. Solutions of barium chloride and aluminum sulfate are mixed.

_____

5. Solid copper(II) hydroxide decomposes.

_____

Mass and mole relationships

Now that we can write a formula, we need to be able to calculate formula and molecular mass. This is important so the skill of dimensional analysis with balanced equations can be practiced.

Calculating formula and molecular mass

To calculate a formula mass, we need the periodic table. The formula NaCl is composed of one sodium atom and one chlorine atom. On the periodic table, Na has a mass of 22.99 amu and Cl has a mass of 35.45 amu; adding these together gives the mass of one unit of NaCl as 58.44 amu. Some chemists now use the dalton (Da) as the term for the atomic mass unit. We will use the amu. Sulfur trioxide, SO_3, is made of one sulfur atom and three oxygen atoms and has a molecular mass of 32.07 amu + 3(16.00) amu = 80.07 amu.

Why was a different term for the mass used? There is a difference between formula mass and molecular mass. Formula mass is the term used when the atoms are held together by an ionic bond, and molecular mass is the term used for a molecule held together by covalent bonds. In general, if the compound has a metal and a nonmetal in it, it has a formula mass, and if it is composed of only nonmetals, it has a molecular mass.

EXERCISE 7·1

Indicate if you are determining the formula or molecular mass of each of the following substances and then record the calculated value.

	TYPE OF MASS	CALCULATED VALUE
1. MgO	_____	_____
2. N_2O_5	_____	_____
3. CaF_2	_____	_____
4. CCl_4	_____	_____
5. $AlPO_4$	_____	_____
6. Ag_2CO_3	_____	_____
7. $Au_2(C_2O_4)_3$	_____	_____

8. HgO _____ _____

9. HF _____ _____

10. NH_3 _____ _____

11. SO_3 _____ _____

12. Na_2SO_4 _____ _____

13. $Cu(NO_3)_2$ _____ _____

14. $BaCO_3$ _____ _____

15. $(NH_4)_3PO_4$ _____ _____

16. KCl _____ _____

17. H_2SO_4 _____ _____

18. CO _____ _____

19. KOH _____ _____

20. $Mg_3(PO_4)_2$ _____ _____

Calculating molar mass

In chemistry experiments the mass of objects is measured in grams—so how many grams are in 58.44 amu? Using the conversion factor of 1 amu to 1.661×10^{-24} g,

$$58.44 \text{ amu} \times \frac{1.661 \times 10^{-24} \text{ g}}{1 \text{ amu}} = 9.707 \times 10^{-23} \text{ g}.$$

This number is so small, our balances can't mass it! A typical balance will measure to one hundredth of a gram. So how do we mass substances? If a larger number of each species are used and always the same number of them, they can compare on a larger scale. This is similar to using the word *dozen* to represent 12 of anything. The word *dozen* represents 12 of something, such as a dozen eggs or a dozen oranges. But to get a mass big enough to measure in chemistry, a dozen won't do.

We use a number called Avogadro's number, which is equal to 6.022×10^{23} particles of a substance; this is called the mole (or 1 mol). (Why such a strange number? The French chemist Jean Baptiste Perrin experimentally determined the number of atoms in 32 g of oxygen molecules.) So the word *mole* is like the word *dozen*—it represents a certain number of things. There is a unique relationship between the amu of one formula unit and the mass of a mole:

$$58.44 \text{ amu} \times \frac{1.661 \times 10^{-24} \text{ g}}{1 \text{ amu}} \times \frac{6.022 \times 10^{23}}{1 \text{ mol}} = 58.44 \text{ g/mol}.$$

What does this mean? If we add a formula unit of a species we get an answer in daltons; if we add a mole of them, the numeric value *is the same* but the unit is g/mol. This means we do not have to do conversions from amu to grams and then to moles in every problem. We simply need to know if we are adding the mass of one unit (amu) or 1 mole of them to choose the proper label. The mass of 1 mole is called molar mass and is given the units of g/mol or gmol^{-1}.

Calculate the molar mass of the following substances. Save your work—it will help with Exercise 7-3.

1. CO _____

2. SiO_2 _____

3. N_2O_3 _____

4. $CuSO_4$ _____

5. $(NH_4)_3PO_3$ _____

6. NO _____

7. $NaOH$ _____

8. FeS _____

9. $CuCl_2$ _____

10. $Cu(OH)_2$ _____

11. I_2 _____

12. N_2O_4 _____

13. $(NH_4)_2SO_4$ _____

14. HNO_2 _____

15. H_2O _____

16. O_2 _____

17. $AgC_2H_3O_2$ _____

18. MgS _____

19. N_2O_5 _____

20. $Ca(OH)_2$ _____

Calculating percent composition

The percent composition is the relative amount of each atom in the compound. No matter the amount of a compound present, the percent of each atom making up the compound remains the same. To calculate the percent composition, there are four simple steps:

1. Find the total mass of each atom in one unit of the compound.

2. Find the molar mass of the compound.

3. Divide each atom's mass by the molar mass.

4. Multiply by 100.

$$\% \text{ of each atom} = \frac{\# \text{ of each atom} \times \text{mass of the atom}}{\text{molar mass of the compound}} \times 100$$

Double-check by adding the percentages together. The total should be 100.

Sample Problem 1: In our sodium chloride example from before, sodium contributed 22.99 g/mol and chlorine contributed 35.45 g/mol to the total molar mass of 58.44 g/mol. Find the percent composition of NaCl.

$$\% \text{ of Na} = \frac{1 \times 22.99 \text{ g}}{58.44 \text{ g/mol}} \times 100$$

$$\% \text{ of Na} = 39.34\%$$

$$\% \text{ of Cl} = \frac{1 \times 35.45 \text{ g}}{58.44 \text{ g/mol}} \times 100$$

$$\% \text{ of Cl} = 60.66\%$$

Double-check: 39.34% + 60.66% = 100%.

Sample Problem 2: If we have a 155.0 g sample of sodium chloride, how many grams are Na and how many are Cl? NaCl?

Using our percentages we can determine how many grams of the sample are sodium atoms and how many grams are chlorine atoms. Sodium is 39.34% of the sample, or 155.0 × 0.3934 = 60.98 g, and chlorine is 60.66% of the sample, or 155.0 × 0.6066 = 94.02 g.

Sample Problem 3: What is the percent composition of each atom in calcium phosphate, $Ca_3(PO_4)_2$?

In this formula there are three calcium atoms, each with a mass of 40.08 g/mol, two phosphorus atoms, each with a mass of 30.97 g/mol, and eight oxygen atoms, each with a mass of 16.00 g/mol.

$$\% \text{ of Ca} = \frac{3 \times 40.08 \text{ g}}{310.18 \text{ g/mol}} \times 100$$

$$\% \text{ of Ca} = 38.76\%$$

$$\% \text{ of P} = \frac{2 \times 30.97 \text{ g}}{310.18 \text{ g/mol}} \times 100$$

$$\% \text{ of P} = 19.97\%$$

$$\% \text{ of O} = \frac{8 \times 16.00}{310.18 \text{ g/mol}} \times 100$$

$$\% \text{ of O} = 41.27\%$$

Double-check: 38.76% + 19.97% + 41.27% = 100%.

Calculate the percentage of each atom in the following substances.

1. CO _____

2. SiO_2 _____

3. N_2O_3 _____

4. $CuSO_4$ _____

5. $(NH_4)_3PO_3$ _____

6. NO _____

7. NaOH _____

8. FeS _____

9. $CuCl_2$ _____

10. $Cu(OH)_2$ _____

11. I_2 _____

12. N_2O_4 _____

13. $(NH_4)_2SO_4$ _____

14. HNO_2 _____

15. H_2O _____

16. O_2 _____

17. $AgC_2H_3O_2$ _____

18. MgS _____

19. N_2O_5 _____

20. $Ca(OH)_2$ _____

Molar conversions between grams and particles

Do we always mass one mole? No! We need to practice changing different amounts of a substance into moles and converting moles into grams. We can also calculate how many particles we have. The particles could be molecules, ions, or formula units, depending on the species given.

To convert grams to moles, the given grams are divided by the molar mass. Set up in dimensional analysis, it looks like this:

$$\text{given grams of substance} \times \frac{1 \text{ mol of substance}}{\text{molar mass of substance}} = \text{moles of substance.}$$

To convert from moles to grams, the setup looks like this:

$$\text{given moles of substance} \times \frac{\text{molar mass of substance}}{1 \text{ mol of substance}} = \text{grams of substance.}$$

Figure 7.1 shows the conversion relationships between grams and moles.

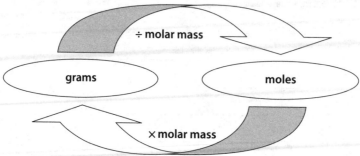

Figure 7.1

If we want to convert between particles and moles, we need to use Avogadro's number in the ratio. Converting from moles to particles looks like this:

$$\text{given moles of substance} \times \frac{6.022 \times 10^{23} \text{ particles}}{1 \text{ mol of substance}} = \text{particles of substance.}$$

The conversion from particles to moles looks like this:

$$\text{given particles of substance} \times \frac{1 \text{ mol of substance}}{6.022 \times 10^{23} \text{ particles}} = \text{moles of substance.}$$

Figure 7.2 shows the conversion relationships between moles and particles.

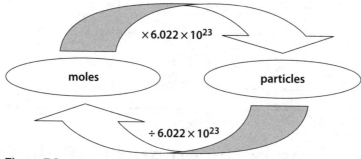

Figure 7.2

It is a good idea to draw a plan of the steps that need to be taken to solve a problem. Combining the steps above, we can draw one map to make a plan for any of these conversions (see Figure 7.3).

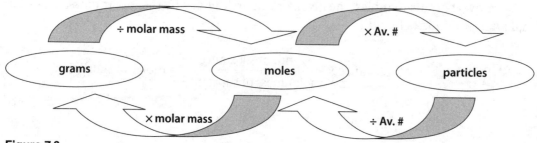

Figure 7.3

One additional step is to change to atoms from particles (see Figure 7.4). This requires knowing the number of atoms in the particle. For instance, the number of atoms in carbon dioxide, CO_2, is three. If we only want to know how many oxygen atoms are present in the particles of CO_2, we would use 2 in the conversion.

$$\text{number of particles} \times \frac{\text{number of atoms}}{1 \text{ particle}} = \text{number of atoms}$$

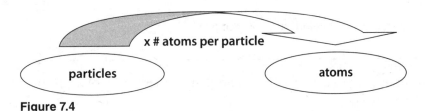

Figure 7.4

Sample Problem 4: Given 71.4 g of $Mg_3(PO_4)_2$, how many moles are present?

First we need to calculate the molar mass of $Mg_3(PO_4)_2$. From the periodic table we find that magnesium is 24.31 gmol⁻¹, phosphorus is 30.97 gmol⁻¹, and oxygen is 16.00 gmol⁻¹.

$$(24.31 \text{ gmol}^{-1} \times 3) + (30.97 \text{ gmol}^{-1} \times 2) + (16.00 \text{ gmol}^{-1} \times 8) = 262.87 \text{ gmol}^{-1}$$

$$71.4 \text{ g } Mg_3(PO_4)_2 \times \frac{1 \text{ mol } Mg_3(PO_4)_2}{262.87 \text{ g } Mg_3(PO_4)_2} = 0.272 \text{ mol } Mg_3(PO_4)_2$$

Sample Problem 5: Given 1.58 mol of $Mg_3(PO4)_2$, how many grams are present?

$$1.58 \text{ mol } Mg_3(PO_4)_2 \times \frac{262.87 \text{ g } Mg_3(PO_4)_2}{1 \text{ mol } Mg_3(PO_4)_2} = 415 \text{ g } Mg_3(PO_4)_2$$

Sample Problem 6: Given 97.3 g of $Mg_3(PO_4)_2$, how many particles of $Mg_3(PO_4)_2$ are present?

This is a two-step problem:

$$97.3 \text{ g } Mg_3(PO_4)_2 \times \frac{1 \text{ mol } Mg_3(PO_4)_2}{262.87 \text{ g } Mg_3(PO_4)_2} \times \frac{6.022 \times 10^{23} \text{ particles}}{1 \text{ mol } Mg_3(PO_4)_2} = 2.23 \times 10^{23} \text{ particles } Mg_3(PO_4)_2$$

Sample Problem 7: Given 23.8 g of $Ca_3(PO_4)_2$, how many atoms of oxygen are present?

$$23.8 \text{ g } Ca_3(PO_4)_2 \times \frac{1 \text{ mol } Ca_3(PO_4)_2}{310.18 \text{ g } Ca_3(PO_4)_2} \times \frac{6.022 \times 10^{23} \text{ particles}}{1 \text{ mol } Ca_3(PO_4)_2}$$

$$= 4.62 \times 10^{22} \text{ particles } Ca_3(PO_4)_2 \times \frac{8 \text{ atoms of O}}{1 \text{ particle } Ca_3(PO_4)_2}$$

$$= 3.70 \times 10^{23} \text{ atoms of O}$$

Solve the following problems.

1. Given 4.62 mol of sodium hydroxide, NaOH, how many grams are present?

2. If there are 5.13 g of NaOH, how many moles are present?

3. How many particles are present in 79.8 g of NaOH?

4. How many grams of potassium sulfide are present if there are 1.79×10^{24} particles present? Yes, find the formula first!

5. How many atoms of chlorine are present in 1.50 mol of chlorine gas, Cl_2?

6. How many atoms of oxygen are present in 37.8 g of calcium carbonate? Yes, find the formula first!

7. How many moles are in 32.0 g of SO_2?

8. Calculate the grams present in 4.00 mol of KI.

9. Calculate the number of moles in 68.0 g of Na_2S.

10. Calculate the mass in grams of 2.49×10^{21} molecules of water.

11. Calculate the number of formula units in 10.0 g of K_2SO_4.

12. Calculate the number of atoms in 32.0 grams of oxygen gas, O_2.

13. Calculate the number of moles in 6.43×10^{22} molecules of SO_2.

14. Calculate the number of grams in 12.0 mol of S.

15. Calculate the total number of atoms in 2.74 mol of NaCl.

_____

16. Calculate how many carbon atoms are present in 2.55 mol of CO_2.

_____

17. Calculate how many nitrogen atoms are present in 13.8 g of $Ca(NO_3)_2$.

_____

18. Calculate the number of moles in 55.5 g of Al.

_____

19. Calculate the number of moles in 89.3 g of $MgSO_4$.

_____

20. Calculate the number of bromine atoms in 149.0 g of Br_2.

_____

Stoichiometry

Stoichiometry is a big word for expressing the number of particles to a mass by using dimensional analysis with moles. You need a _balanced_ equation and sharpened math skills! Problems can be asked in a variety of ways, but one of the steps will require changing from moles of one species to moles of another species by using a balanced equation. The plot thickens! Yes, you need several skills you have already learned: calculating molar masses, doing dimensional analysis, and balancing equations. Thanks to the understanding that a chemical equation such as

$$2Na + Cl_2 \rightarrow 2NaCl$$

can be expressed as "two moles of sodium atoms combined with one mole of chlorine molecules can make two moles of sodium chloride," the balanced equation gives us the _ratio_ between species in moles! The ratio used depends on what is asked; the ratio needs to be written so the substance you are changing from is on the bottom, to cancel, and the substance you are changing to is on the top. For instance, the ratio $\dfrac{1 \text{ mol Cl}_2}{2 \text{ mol NaCl}}$ could also be written

$$\dfrac{2 \text{ mol NaCl}}{1 \text{ mol Cl}_2},$$

depending on the problem being solved. Looking at Figure 7.5, once moles of the starting substance are calculated, this can be multiplied by the ratio from the balanced equation, where the coefficient of the starting material is on the bottom and the coefficient of the substance being converted to is on the top, giving you the moles of the new substance.

$$\boxed{\text{Moles of A}} \times \frac{\text{coefficient of B}}{\text{coefficient of A}} = \boxed{\text{Moles of B}}$$

Figure 7.5

EXERCISE
7·5

Write expressions describing the relationships between moles of reactants and moles of products.
For example, $\dfrac{1\,mol\,O_2}{2\,mol\,H_2O}$ *is one relationship for the equation* $2H_2(g) + O_2(g) \rightarrow 2H_2O(g)$.

1. $N_2(g) + 3H_2(g) \rightarrow 2NH_3(g)$

2. $CH_4(g) + 2O_2(g) \rightarrow CO_2(g) + 2H_2O(g)$

3. $Na_2CO_3(s) + 2HCl(aq) \rightarrow 2NaCl(aq) + H_2O(l) + CO_2(g)$

4. $2Na(s) + Cl_2(g) \rightarrow 2NaCl(s)$

5. $Cl_2(g) + 2KBr(aq) \rightarrow 2KCl(aq) + Br_2(l)$

Using this skill, we can convert from one species to another. Now you are ready for stoichiometry!

Mole-to-mole conversions

To do a conversion, we always need a balanced equation. Then we look at the problem to find out what two species need to be in the ratio. Then set up the ratio so units cancel.

- ◆ Write a balanced equation.
- ◆ Read the problem for the species being used.
- ◆ Set up the ratio so units cancel.

Sample Problem 8:   Using $2Na + Cl_2 \rightarrow 2NaCl$, if we have 2 mol of sodium and excess chlorine, how many moles of sodium chloride can we make?

The ratio between sodium and sodium chloride in the balanced equation is 2:2.

$$2 \text{ mol of Na} \times \frac{2 \text{ mol NaCl}}{2 \text{ mol Na}} = 2 \text{ mol NaCl}$$

EXERCISE
7·6

Use the equation $4Fe(s) + 3O_2(g) \rightarrow 2Fe_2O_3(s)$ to answer the following questions.

1. How many moles of O_2 do we need to react with 56 mol of Fe?

2. If all 56 mol of Fe from question 1 react, how many moles of Fe_2O_3 are produced?

3. How many moles of Fe are necessary to make 25 mol of Fe_2O_3?

_____

4. How many moles of O_2 are required to make 32 mol of Fe_2O_3?

_____

5. If 120 mol of O_2 is used, how many moles of Fe_2O_3 could be made?

_____

6. How many moles of Fe are necessary to react completely with 66 mol of O_2?

_____

7. Calculate the number of moles of O_2 needed to react with 2.7 mol of Fe.

_____

8. Calculate the number of moles of Fe_2O_3 formed if 7.7 mol of Fe fully reacts.

_____

9. Calculate the number of moles of each reactant needed to form 5.8 mol of product.

_____

10. Calculate the number of moles of product formed if 2.7 mol of O_2 reacts with excess Fe.

_____

Other stoichiometric calculations

A variety of problems arise if you are given a unit other than moles to start with, and you want to convert to a unit other than moles. However, in all cases the important step is the stoichiometry step of converting from moles of a given substance to moles of a needed substance. Here are some samples of other types of problems, with a chance to practice them. Use the following equation for sample problems 9 and 10:

$$Cu(s) + 2AgNO_3(aq) \rightarrow 2Ag(s) + Cu(NO_3)_2(aq)$$

Sample Problem 9: Given 32.1 g of Cu, how many grams of Ag can be made?

$$32.1 \text{ g Cu} \times \frac{1 \text{ mol Cu}}{63.55 \text{ g}} \times \frac{2 \text{ mol Ag}}{1 \text{ mol Cu}} \times \frac{107.9 \text{ g Ag}}{1 \text{ mol Ag}} = 109 \text{ g Ag}$$

Sample Problem 10: If 45.0 g of Ag needs to be produced, how many moles of Cu are needed?

$$45.0 \text{ g Ag} \times \frac{1 \text{ mol Ag}}{107.9 \text{ g Ag}} \times \frac{1 \text{ mol Cu}}{2 \text{ mol Ag}} = 0.209 \text{ mol Cu}$$

As you can see from these two problems, the ratios are arranged so units cancel and only the desired units remain. In the first problem, the silver was on the top in the ratio, and in the second problem it was on the bottom. Specifics of gas stoichiometry and solution stoichiometry will be covered in Chapters 8 and 9.

EXERCISE
7·7

Using the equation $2Al(s) + 6HNO_3(aq) \rightarrow 2Al(NO_3)_3(aq) + 3H_2(g)$, answer the following questions.

1. How many grams of Al react completely with 12.0 mol of nitric acid?

   _____

2. If 3.45 mol of Al reacts with excess nitric acid, how many grams of $Al(NO_3)_3$ are produced?

   _____

3. How many grams of H_2 are produced from 15.7 g of Al reacting with an excess of nitric acid?

   _____

4. If 0.750 mol of $Al(NO_3)_3$ is needed, how many grams of HNO_3 are required if plenty of Al is available?

   _____

5. If 9.82 g of Al reacts with excess HNO_3, how many grams of $Al(NO_3)_3$ are made?

   _____

6. How many moles of Al are necessary to react completely with 65.3 g of HNO_3?

   _____

7. If 5.34×10^{23} atoms of Al are present in excess nitric acid, how many grams of H_2 can be formed?

   _____

8. How many grams of aluminum are required to completely react with excess nitric acid to form 13.0 g of aluminum nitrate?

   _____

9. If 5.34×10^{22} molecules of hydrogen gas are formed, how many atoms of aluminum are needed?

   _____

10. How many grams of aluminum nitrate are formed if 10.0 g of nitric acid reacts with excess aluminum?

    _____

11. If excess nitric acid reacts with 2.4 mol of aluminum, how many molecules of hydrogen gas are formed?

    _____

12. What mass of aluminum is needed to fully react with 57.0 g of nitric acid?

    _____

13. Calculate the number of grams of aluminum nitrate that can be formed if excess aluminum reacts with 3.74 mol of nitric acid.

14. Calculate the moles formed of each product if excess nitric acid reacts with 12.7 g of Al.

15. To form 374 mol of H_2, how many atoms of Al are needed with excess nitric acid?

Limiting reagents

In the problems so far, one of the reactants has been in excess, so the limiting reagent has always been known. The limiting reagent is the reactant that, because of its "limited" amount, limits the amount of product that can be made. From this point on these two terms, *limiting reagent* or *limiting reactant*, will be used to describe the chemical limiting the amount of product produced. The problems now are going to differ in that both reactants will have a given amount and we will have to determine which one is limiting. *This means two stoichiometry problems per question!*

There are multiple ways to up these problems, depending on how the question is asked. Always doing them as two full stoichiometry problems often answers two questions: (1) which reactant is the limiting reagent, and (2) how much product can be made. Whichever reactant makes the smallest amount of product is the limiting reagent, since it will all be used and limits how much product can be made!

Sample Problem 11: Using the equation $2H_2(g) + O_2(g) \rightarrow 2H_2O(l)$, given 37.4 g of H_2 and 50.7 g of O_2, identify the limiting reagent and calculate the number of grams of water made.

Remember to first calculate the molar masses of H_2, O_2, and H_2O, and set up the ratios being used to cancel units.

$$37.4 \text{ g } H_2 \times \frac{1 \text{ mol } H_2}{2.016 \text{ g } H_2} \times \frac{2 \text{ mol } H_2O}{2 \text{ mol } H_2} \times \frac{18.02 \text{ g } H_2O}{1 \text{ mol } H_2O} = 334 \text{ g } H_2O$$

$$50.7 \text{ g } O_2 \times \frac{1 \text{ mol } O_2}{32.00 \text{ g } O_2} \times \frac{2 \text{mol } H_2O}{1 \text{ mol } O_2} \times \frac{18.02 \text{ g } H_2O}{1 \text{ mol } H_2O} = 57.1 \text{ g } H_2O$$

The O_2 made less water, so it is the limiting reagent, and the amount of product that can be made is 57.1 g of H_2O. Don't be tricked by thinking the one with fewer grams at the start is limiting!

EXERCISE
7·8

Using the equation $Zn(s) + 2HCl(aq) \rightarrow ZnCl_2(aq) + H_2(g)$ and the information given in each problem, determine which reactant is the limiting reagent and how much zinc chloride (in grams) is produced in each problem.

1. 2.50 g of Zn is added to 5.00 g of HCl.

2. 10.0 g of Zn is added to 10.0 g of HCl.

3. 16.3 g of Zn is added to 8.15 g of HCl.

_____

4. 1.2×10^{22} atoms of Zn are added to 15.00 g of HCl.

_____

5. 2.3 mol of Zn reacts with 2.3 mol of HCl.

_____

6. 2.7 mol of Zn is added to 34.0 g of HCl.

_____

7. 34.7 g of Zn is added to 3.42×10^{22} formula units of HCl.

_____

8. 4.5 mol of Zn reacts with 12.3 g of HCl.

_____

9. 12.45 g of Zn reacts with 37.4 g of HCl.

_____

10. 3.7×10^{23} atoms of Zn are added to 4.7×10^{23} formula units of HCl.

_____

Percent yield

For a variety of reasons, when reactions occur they often do not make the amount expected. The amount calculated through stoichiometry is the maximum yield, 100%. Percent yield is a ratio of how many grams are actually made (actual yield) in comparison to the maximum amount (in grams) that could have been made (expected or theoretical yield), expressed as a percentage.

$$\frac{\text{grams of actual yield}}{\text{grams of theoretical yield}} \times 100 = \text{percent yield}$$

Sample Problem 12: If the expected yield is 42.1 g of S and 28.3 g S is actually made, what is the percent yield?

$$\frac{28.3 \text{ g S}}{42.1 \text{ g S}} \times 100 = 67.2\%$$

Don't forget to use significant figures!

Perform the following calculations.

1. If 42.6 g of ammonia is made in a reaction where 55.0 g is expected, what is the percent yield?

2. If a reaction consistently has an 85% yield, and 23.7 g of the product is made, what is the theoretical yield of the product?

3. In the reaction $2NaOH(aq) + NiSO_4(aq) \rightarrow Ni(OH)_2(s) + Na_2SO_4(aq)$, with an excess of $NiSO_4$, what is the percent yield if 20.0 g of NaOH makes 12.5 g of $Ni(OH)_2$?

4. If 40.0 g of N_2 reacts with 20.0 g of H_2 to make 45.9 g of NH_3 in the reaction $N_2(g) + 3H_2(g) \rightarrow 2NH_3(g)$, what is the percent yield of NH_3?

5. Calculate the percent yield if 34.0 g of a single product is expected but only 26.9 g is formed.

6. If 82.0 g of N_2 reacts with 40.0 g of H_2 to make 45.9 g of NH_3 in the reaction $N_2(g) + 3H_2(g) \rightarrow 2NH_3(g)$, what is the percent yield of NH_3?

7. Calculate the percent yield if a reaction forms 82.0 g of product when 96.0 g is expected.

8. If 2.7×10^{23} molecules of ammonia are made in a reaction where 3.4×10^{23} molecules were expected, what was the percent yield?

9. If 2.4 mol of ammonia are made in a reaction where 3.7 mol were expected, what was the percent yield?

10. If 3.72×10^{22} molecules of ammonia are made in a reaction where 1.5 mol were expected, what was the percent yield?

EXERCISE

7·10

Answer the following questions.

1. What is the difference between formula mass and molecular mass?

2. What is the difference between formula/molecular mass and molar mass?

3. Calculate the formula mass of:

   a. $CaCl_2$ _____

   b. AgI   _____

   c. Fe_2O_3 _____

4. Calculate the molecular mass of:

   a. HF   _____

   b. NI_3 _____

   c. P_4O_{10} _____

5. Calculate the molar mass of:

   a. Barium nitride (Ba_3N_2)   _____

   b. Dinitrogen pentoxide (N_2O_5)   _____

   c. Potassium permanganate ($KMnO_4$)   _____

6. Using $Al_2(SO_4)_3$, find the following:

   a. How many grams are in 3.00 mol of $Al_2(SO_4)_3$?

   _____

   b. How many moles are in 157 g of $Al_2(SO_4)_3$?

   _____

   c. How many formula units are in 157 g of $Al_2(SO_4)_3$?

   _____

   d. How many grams are in 9.72×10^{25} formula units of $Al_2(SO_4)_3$?

   _____

7. According to the reaction $CuSO_4(aq) + Zn(s) \rightarrow Cu(s) + ZnSO_4(aq)$, how many grams of copper can be produced from 3.16 g of zinc with an excess of $CuSO_4$?

   _____

8. If 5.25 g of nitrogen gas reacts with 7.52 g of hydrogen gas to make ammonia in the reaction $N_2(g) + 3H_2(g) \rightarrow 2NH_3(g)$, answer the following:

   a. What is the limiting reactant?   _____

   b. How much product is made?   _____

   c. How much leftover reactant is present?   _____

9. In a reaction where 82.1 g of product is expected but only 46.3 g is produced, what is the percent yield?

   _____

10. What is the percent yield of Ag_2CO_3 if 25.0 g of $AgNO_3$ reacts with 25.0 g of Na_2CO_3 according to the reaction $2AgNO_3(aq) + Na_2CO_3(aq) \rightarrow Ag_2CO_3(s) + 2NaNO_3(aq)$ and 18.8 g of Ag_2CO_3 is actually produced?

   _____

Gas laws

8

Gases are a unique group of substances. With particles normally far apart, they can be compressed into a smaller volume by reducing the amount of space between particles. This capability makes for interesting relationships between volume, temperature, and pressure for a gas. *Volume* of course is the space a gas occupies, *temperature* is a measure of the average kinetic energy of the particles of a gas, and *pressure* is the amount of force applied by the particles to a given area. The volume of a gas is normally given in *liters* (L), temperature in *degrees Celsius* (°C), and pressure in *atmospheres* (atm). Another common pressure unit is millimeters of mercury (mmHg), which is also called a torr. When comparing pressure units, it will be useful to know that 1.00 atm is equivalent to 760 mmHg and 760 torr. To change from units in torr to atm, divide the given torr by 760 torr.

In all calculations involving gases, the temperatures *must* be converted to a unit called the kelvin. This conversion will be shown later. When working problems, make sure the units on both sides of the equation are the same! As we look at the laws about gases, the first laws will hold one unit constant so the relationship between the other two units can be observed.

In many gas problems, the amount of gas in the problem is fixed. However, in other problems the amount may be changed by adding or removing some of the gas, or by a gas mixture reacting chemically to form new products, or by gas leaking out of its container. It is vital to establish which of these situations is involved when working a gas problem.

Volume and pressure (Boyle's law)

When temperature remains constant, if additional pressure is applied to a gas the volume will decrease, assuming a fixed amount of gas is present. Think of a capped syringe—when the plunger is pushed in (pressure is increased), the plunger decreases the volume of gas in the syringe. This relationship is represented by the equation $P_1V_1 = P_2V_2$. When one value goes up, the other must correspondingly go down; if the pressure doubles, the volume is cut in half! This type of relationship is inversely proportional. On a graph, a straight line will not be shown until the inverse relationship is graphed.

The data points listed in the following table are graphed in Figure 8.1.

Pressure in atm	Volume in L
1.0	3.0
1.5	2.0
2.0	1.5
2.5	1.2
3.0	1.0
3.5	0.86
4.0	0.75
4.5	0.67
5.0	0.60

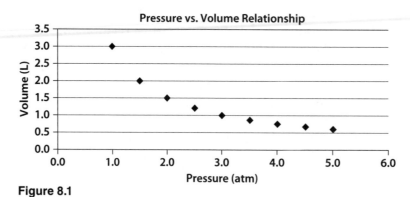

Figure 8.1

When the inverse of one of the sets of data is found—by taking 1 divided by the measurement—and graphed, the resulting graph shows a linear relationship. (See the data points listed in the following table, and the resulting graph, Figure 8.2.)

Pressure in atm	1/volume in L
1.0	0.33
1.5	0.50
2.0	0.67
2.5	0.83
3.0	1.0
3.5	1.16
4.0	1.33
4.5	1.50
5.0	1.67

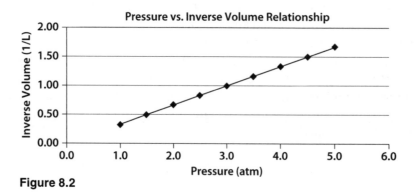

Figure 8.2

This indicates the inverse relationship of pressure and volume. Will the volume ever become zero? No, because gas molecules take up space, and eventually, if enough pressure is applied, the gas molecules will become close enough to one another to attract other molecules and turn into a liquid.

The following sample problems all assume there is a fixed amount of gas present. In these types of problems, three measurements will be given and the fourth one will be the unknown. To keep from getting confused, always make a list of P_1, P_2, V_1, and V_2. Then substitute into the equation $P_1V_1 = P_2V_2$.

Sample Problem 1: A gas occupies 2.1 L at a pressure of 1.2 atm. If the gas is in a flexible container at constant temperature, what is the new volume if the pressure decreases to 0.82 atm?

$$P_1 = 1.2 \text{ atm}, P_2 = 0.82 \text{ atm, and } V_1 = 2.1 \text{ L}; V_2 \text{ is unknown}$$

$$(1.2 \text{ atm}) \times (2.1 \text{ L}) = (0.82 \text{ atm}) \times (V_2)$$

$$V_2 = 3.1 \text{ L}$$

> Concept check: the pressure decreases from 1.2 atm to 0.81 atm, so the volume should increase. Is 3.1 L larger than 2.1 L? Yes, it is! So this answer is reasonable.

Sample Problem 2: A gas with a volume of 5.8 L at a pressure of 1.1 atm expands to 6.9 L at constant temperature. What is the new pressure?

$$P_1 = 1.1 \text{ atm, } V_1 = 5.8 \text{ L, and } V_2 = 6.9 \text{ L}; P_2 \text{ is unknown}$$

$$(1.1 \text{ atm}) \times (5.8 \text{ L}) = P_2 \times (6.9 \text{ L})$$

$$P_2 = 0.92 \text{ atm}$$

> Concept check: the volume is increasing from 5.8 L to 6.9 L. What should be happening to the pressure? It should be decreasing. Is 0.92 atm less than 1.1 atm? Yes, it is, so this answer is also reasonable.

EXERCISE
8·1

Use the given conditions to solve for the unknowns. Assume that the amount of gas present and the temperature remain constant. Be sure to check your answer for reasonableness.

1. A container with the ability to expand and contract has its pressure changed from 5.0 atm to 7.5 atm. If the original volume is 4.0 L, what is the new volume?

_____

2. A container of gas has a pressure of 2.76 atm. The volume of gas in the container expands from 10.0 L to 15.0 L. What is the new pressure?

_____

3. What is the original volume of a container if the pressure changes from 1.25 atm to 3.00 atm and the final volume is 9.90 L?

_____

4. If the final pressure in a container is 6.10 atm and the volume changes from 2.5 L to 3.7 L, what is the original pressure?

_____

5. If a gas occupies 275 cm³ at 1.2 atm, what is its volume at 2.4 atm?

_____

6. If the volume of a gas doubles, what happens to the pressure?

_____

7. If the pressure of a gas doubles, what happens to the volume?

_____

8. If 2.4 L of gas is at a pressure of 1.0 atm, what is the volume when the pressure is raised to 3.0 atm?

_____

9. The pressure of a gas changes from 3.0 to 1.0 atms. What is the new volume if the original volume is 22.4 L?

_____

10. If the volume of a gas is originally 1.5 L at a pressure of 0.900 atm, what is the new pressure when the volume is changed to 1.2 L?

_____

Volume and temperature

When pressure remains constant, if the temperature is increased the volume of the gas will increase, assuming a fixed amount of gas is present. The gas molecules will be hitting the walls of the container with an increased average kinetic energy; to keep the same pressure, the volume must expand. This relationship is represented by the equation

$$\frac{V_1}{T_1} = \frac{V_2}{T_2}.$$

When one value increases, the other value must also increase! Doubling the temperature means the volume doubles! This is called a direct relationship, and if graphed it will show a linear relationship. Graphing the data in the following table results in Figure 8.3.

Temperature in K	Volume in L
250	5.0
300	6.0
350	7.0
400	8.0
450	9.0
500	10.0
550	11.0
600	12.0

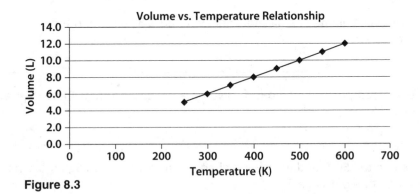

Figure 8.3

Be careful, though: changing the temperature from 25°C to 50°C is not doubling the temperature! Temperatures *must* be expressed in kelvins (K). The Kelvin temperature scale has all temperatures adjusted to positive values; the lowest possible temperature is 0 K. The conversion from degrees Celsius to kelvins is to add 273 to the Celsius temperature. So instead of 25°C to 50°C, the temperature has changed only from 298 K to 323 K—which is *not* doubled! Doubling the temperature from 300 K to 600 K would be necessary to double the volume.

The sample problems that follow all assume a fixed amount of gas is present.

Sample Problem 3: If a 25.0 L volume of CO_2 is heated from 25°C to 88°C at constant pressure, what is the new volume of the gas?

$V_1 = 25.0$ L, $T_1 = 25°C + 273 = 298$ K, and $T_2 = 88°C + 273 = 361$ K; V_2 is unknown

$$\frac{25.0 \text{ L}}{298 \text{ K}} = \frac{V_2}{361 \text{ K}}$$

$$V_2 = 30.3 \text{ L}$$

Concept check: the temperature increases from 298 K to 361 K, so the volume should increase. Is 30.3 L larger than 25.0 L? Yes, it is! So this answer is reasonable.

Sample Problem 4: If a 36.0 L volume of methane at constant pressure and 75°C compresses to a volume of 18.0 L, what is the final temperature?

$V_1 = 36.0$ L, $V_2 = 18.0$ L, and $T_1 = 75°C + 273 = 348$ K; T_2 is unknown

$$\frac{25.0 \text{ L}}{348 \text{ K}} = \frac{18.0 \text{ L}}{V_2}$$

$$T_2 = 251 \text{ K or } 251 - 273 = -22°C$$

Concept check: the volume decreases from 25.0 L to 18.0 L, so the temperature should decrease. Is 251 K smaller than 348 K? Yes, it is! So this answer is reasonable.

EXERCISE
8·2

Use the given conditions to solve for the unknown. Assume that the amount of gas present and the pressure remain constant. Be sure to check your answer for reasonableness.

1. If a 1.2 L volume of gas is cooled from 25°C to 0.°C, what is the final volume?

2. What is the original volume of a gas if its final volume is 38.6 L when the temperature drops from 100°C to 25°C?

3. What is the final temperature of a gas if its volume increases from 6.4 L to 9.2 L and its initial temperature is 35°C?

4. If a gas is heated to 150°C and its volume changes from 125 mL to 525 mL, what is the original temperature of the gas?

5. If a 2.4 L volume of gas is cooled from 75°C to 0°C, what is its final volume?

6. If a 1.2 L volume of gas is heated from 0°C to 50°C, what is its final volume?

7. What is the final temperature of a gas if its volume decreases from 6.4 L to 4.2 L when its initial temperature is 55°C?

8. What is the original temperature of a gas if its volume increases from 8.4 L to 15.2 L and its final temperature is 46°C?

9. What is the original volume of a gas if its final volume is 42.1 L when the temperature is raised from 100°C to 150°C?

10. If the final temperature is three times the original, what is the final volume of a gas that originally occupies 2.1 L?

Pressure and temperature

When the volume remains constant, if the temperature is increased the pressure of the gas will increase. This assumes there is a fixed amount of gas present. The gas molecules will be hitting the walls of the container with more net force (more frequently and with greater energy), and since the container is rigid (not expanding), the pressure increases. This relationship is represented by the equation

$$\frac{P_1}{T_1} = \frac{P_2}{T_2}.$$

When one value increases, the other value also increases! As we saw with volume and pressure, this is a direct relationship. Graphing the following data results in Figure 8.4. Since temperature is also involved in this relationship, remember to convert the temperatures from degrees Celsius to kelvins.

Temperature in K	Pressure in atm
250	1.0
375	1.5
500	2.0
625	2.5
750	3.0
875	3.5
1,000	4.0

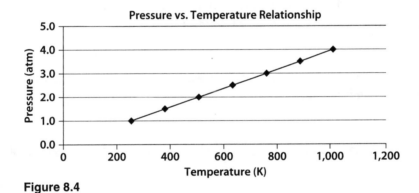

Figure 8.4

The trend line shows the linear relationship. When one value goes up, so does the other, by a corresponding amount.

These sample problems assume a fixed amount gas to be present.

Sample Problem 5: A gas with a pressure of 2.1 atm at 45°C in a rigid container is cooled to 18°C. What is the new pressure of the gas?

$P_1 = 2.1$ atm, $T_1 = 45°C + 273 = 318$ K, and $T_2 = 18°C + 273 = 291$ K; P_2 is unknown

$$\frac{2.1 \text{ atm}}{318 \text{ K}} = \frac{P_2}{291 \text{ K}}$$

$$P_2 = 1.9 \text{ atm}$$

Concept check: the temperature decreased from 318 K to 291 K, so the volume should decrease. Is 1.9 atm smaller than 2.1 atm? Yes, it is! So this answer is reasonable.

Sample Problem 6: A sample of gas at 25°C, 1.0 atm, and constant volume has the pressure raised to 2.0 atm. What is the new temperature?

$$P_1 = 1.0 \text{ atm}, P_2 = 2.0 \text{ atm}, T_1 = 25°C + 273 = 298 \text{ K}; T_2 \text{ is unknown}$$

$$\frac{1.0 \text{ atm}}{298 \text{ K}} = \frac{2.0 \text{ atm}}{T_2}$$

$$T_2 = 596 \text{ K or } 596 \text{ K} - 273 = 323°C$$

Concept check: the pressure increased from 1.0 atm to 2.0 atm, so the temperature should increase. Is 596 K larger than 298 K? Yes, 596/298 = 2, so it is larger by a factor of two! Doubling the pressure doubled the Kelvin temperature. So this answer is reasonable.

EXERCISE
8·3

Use the given conditions to solve for the unknown. Assume that the amount of gas present and the volume remain constant. Be sure to check your answer for reasonableness.

1. A gas at 22°C and 3.5 atm of pressure is cooled to −10°C. What is the final pressure of the gas?

2. The pressure in a cylinder is measured to have risen from 4.7 atm to 12.6 atm. If the original temperature is −78°C, what is the final temperature?

3. What is the initial temperature of a gas if its pressure decreases from 8.2 atm to 6.8 atm and its final temperature is 49°C?

4. If the final pressure in a container is 500 torr when the temperature falls from 300 K to 150 K, what is the initial pressure?

5. If the pressure of a gas doubles, what is the original temperature of the gas, given a final temperature of 22°C?

6. If the temperature of a gas is cut in half, what is the final pressure of the gas, given an original pressure of 1.0 atm?

7. A gas at 82°C and 1.5 atm of pressure is heated to 155°C. What is the final pressure of the gas?

8. If the final pressure in a container is 500 torr after the temperature rises from 100 K to 300 K, what is the initial pressure?

_____

9. What is the initial temperature of a gas if its pressure decreases from 3.3 atm to 2.2 atm and its final temperature is 25°C?

_____

10. If the temperature of a gas is tripled, what is the final pressure of the gas, given an original pressure of 1.0 atm?

_____

Volume and particle number (Avogadro's hypothesis)

When the pressure and temperature of a gas are held constant, the number of particles of gas present is directly proportional to the volume of the gas. This accounts for volume changes as the amount of gas present changes. One mole (Avogadro's number of particles, 6.022×10^{23}) of any gas at standard temperature and pressure (STP) will occupy 22.4 L of space. If we substitute the conditions of STP and 1 mol into the ideal gas equation (defined later), no matter the gas, the volume is 22.4 L.

STP conditions are 1 atm of pressure (760 mmHg) and 0°C (273 K). At STP, one-half a mole of a gas occupies 11.2 L of space. To build consistency so standard conditions are the same for all types of data, some chemists are recognizing standard temperature to be 298 instead and still use 1 atm of pressure, in which case 1 mol of gas occupies 24.6 L.

Sample Problem 7: If 2.5 mol of gas is present at STP, what volume does the gas occupy?

$$2.5 \text{ mol} \times \frac{22.4 \text{ L}}{1 \text{ mol}} = x$$
$$x = 56 \text{ L of gas}$$

Sample Problem 8: If a gas at STP occupies 18.2 L, how many gas particles are present?

$$18.2 \text{ L} \times \frac{1 \text{ mol}}{22.4 \text{ L}} \times \frac{6.022 \times 10^{23}}{1 \text{ mol}} = x$$
$$x = 4.89 \times 10^{23} \text{ gas particles}$$

EXERCISE
8·4

Answer the following questions using the relationships in the previous section.

1. If a reaction produces 4.25 L of gas at STP, how many moles of gas were produced?

_____

2. If 0.75 mol of a gas is needed from a reaction performed at STP, how many liters should be collected?

_____

3. How many atoms of helium are in a 3.00 L balloon that was filled at STP?

_____

4. How many atoms of a gas are in a container of 22.4 L at STP?

_____

5. If 18.7 L of gas is present at STP, how many moles of gas are present?

_____

6. If 2.7×10^{24} molecules of CO_2 are present at STP, how many moles of gas are present?

_____

7. If 11.2 L of gas is present at STP, how many gas molecules are present?

_____

8. If 38.4 g of CO is needed from a reaction performed at STP, how many liters should be collected?

_____

9. If a reaction produces 12.25 L of Cl_2 at STP, how many grams of gas are produced?

_____

10. If a reaction produces 3.50 L of gas at STP, how many moles of gas are produced?

_____

Volume, temperature, and pressure (combined gas law)

All three laws can be combined into one equation:

$$\frac{P_1 V_1}{T_1} = \frac{P_2 V_2}{T_2}.$$

To know what happens as two factors are changing usually requires solving the equation for one condition. Again, since this equation involves temperature, make sure that all temperatures are expressed in kelvins.

Sample Problem 9: A gas at 742 mmHg and 35.0°C occupies a volume of 7.00 L. What is the volume of the gas at STP?

$P_1 = 742$ mmHg (no conversion to atmospheres is required if both pressure units are the same, since they will cancel each other out), $P_2 = 760$ mmHg, $V_1 = 7.00$ L, $T_1 = 35.0°C + 273 = 308$ K, and $T_2 = 0.0°C + 273 = 273$ K; V_2 is unknown. Use $\frac{P_1 V_1}{T_1} = \frac{P_2 V_2}{T_2}$.

$$\frac{(742 \text{ mmHg}) \times (7.00 \text{ L})}{(35.0 + 273 \text{ K})} = \frac{(760 \text{ mmHg}) \times (V_2)}{(0.0 + 273) \text{K}}$$

$$V_2 = 6.06 \text{ L}$$

Sample Problem 10: A gas at 0.980 atm and 25°C occupies a volume of 835 mL. What is the pressure of the gas when the temperature is raised to 50°C and the volume expands to 911 mL?

$$P_1 = 0.980 \text{ atm},\ V_1 = 835 \text{ mL},\ V_2 = 911 \text{ mL},\ T_1 = 25.0°C + 273 = 298 \text{ K, and}$$
$$T_2 = 50.0°C + 273 = 323 \text{ K};\ P_2 \text{ is unknown}$$

$$\frac{(0.980 \text{ atm}) \times (835 \text{ mL})}{(25.0 + 273)\text{K}} = \frac{(P_2) \times (911 \text{ mL})}{(50.0 + 273)\text{K}}$$

$$P_2 = 0.974 \text{ atm}$$

EXERCISE 8·5

Complete the following table by solving for the missing conditions.

	P_1	V_1	T_1	P_2	V_2	T_2
1.	2.00 atm	1.25 L	100°C	1.00 atm	_____	0.0°C
2.	_____	55.5 mL	20.0°C	3.50 atm	101 mL	60.0°C
3.	970 torr	2.1 L	_____	760 torr	4.2 L	25.0°C
4.	1,020 torr	250. mL	45.0°C	_____	326 mL	15.0°C
5.	1.00 atm	_____	273 K	2.0 atm	12.0 L	400 K
6.	_____	2.80 L	25.5°C	750 torr	5.70 L	51.0°C
7.	0.98 atm	18.0 L	250 K	_____	1.65 L	301 K
8.	2.00 atm	1.25 L	200°C	1.500 atm	_____	50.0°C
9.	1.00 atm	18.25 L	100°C	1.00 atm	12.5 L	_____
10.	760 torr	_____	250 K	0.88 atm	188 mL	500.0 K

Density of a gas at STP

If 1 mol of gas at STP occupies 22.4 L of space, then the molar mass divided by 22.4 will equal the density. The equation is

$$d = \frac{M}{22.4 \text{ L}}.$$

Sample Problem 11: What is the density of CO_2 at STP?

$$d = \frac{44.01 \text{ g}}{22.4 \text{ L}}$$
$$x = 1.96 \text{ gL}^{-1}$$

Sample Problem 12: What is the density of pentane (C_5H_{12}) gas at STP?

$$d = \frac{72.146 \text{ g}}{22.4 \text{ L}}$$

$$x = 3.22 \text{ gL}^{-1}$$

EXERCISE

8·6

Answer the following questions.

1. What is the density of nitrogen gas (N_2) at STP?

_____

2. What is the density of sulfur dioxide gas at STP?

_____

3. What is the density of carbon monoxide gas at STP?

_____

4. What is the density of nitrogen dioxide gas at STP?

_____

5. What is the density of dinitrogen pentoxide gas at STP?

_____

Ideal gas law

If the conditions are not at STP, how do we solve for density or any other value, such as a change in the amount of gas? The *ideal gas law* takes the conditions of an ideal gas at any one point in time and relates them to each other in an equation. An ideal gas is one that meets the following two conditions: gas molecules do not exert repulsive or attractive forces between them and the volume of gas particles is a very tiny fraction of the total volume of the container. The equation is

$$PV = nRT.$$

As we have seen in earlier equations, P represents the pressure but in this equation it must be in atmospheres, V is the volume in liters, and T is the temperature in kelvins. The n represents the moles of gas present and R represents the ideal gas constant. The ideal gas constant is $0.0821 \text{ L} \cdot \text{atm} \times \text{K}^{-1} \cdot \text{mol}^{-1}$. All the units for V, P, and T in the equation must match the units in R, i.e., volume in *liters*, pressure in *atmospheres*, and temperature in *kelvins*. There are other values of R if different units are used, but we will use only the one value.

Nonideal conditions when this equation cannot be used are when the gas molecules are coming close enough to each other to have an attraction between them, such as temperatures close to the condensation point where they become a liquid—which are *low temperatures*—and *high pressures*. Under those conditions, a different equation is used to correct for the volume of the gas molecules and the attractive forces between gas molecules. We will not go into that equation here.

Sample Problem 13: A gas at 313 K and 1.5 atm occupies 2.4 L. How many moles of gas are present?

$$(1.5 \text{ atm})(2.4 \text{ L}) = n(0.0821 \text{ L} \cdot \text{atm} \times \text{K}^{-1} \cdot \text{mol}^{-1})(313 \text{ K})$$
$$n = 0.14 \text{ mol}$$

How can we solve for density from $PV = nRT$? The equation needs to be rearranged! Substituting grams mass (m), which must be in grams divided by molar mass (M) for moles (n), the equation becomes $PV = (m/M)RT$. Rearranging this to $M = \dfrac{gRT}{PV}$, also a very useful equation, we can now substitute density (d) for m/V, resulting in the equation $M = \dfrac{dRT}{P}$. Isolating the density on one side results in the equation $d = \dfrac{MP}{RT}$.

Sample Problem 14: What is the molar mass of 2.25 g of gas at 275 K that occupies 1.0 L with a pressure of 0.950 atm?

$$M = \frac{(2.25 \text{ g})\left(\dfrac{0.0821 \text{ L} \cdot \text{atm}}{\text{K} \cdot \text{mol}}\right)(275 \text{ K})}{0.950 \text{ atm}}$$

$$M = 53.5 \text{ g/mol}$$

Sample Problem 15: What is the density of carbon dioxide gas at 1.10 atm and 285 K?

$$d = \frac{\left(44.01 \dfrac{\text{g}}{\text{mol}}\right)(1.10 \text{ atm})}{\left(0.0821 \dfrac{\text{L} \cdot \text{atm}}{\text{K} \cdot \text{mol}}\right)(285 \text{ K})}$$

$$d = 2.07 \frac{\text{g}}{\text{L}}$$

Answer the following questions.

1. What is the molar mass of a gas that occupies 2.0 L at a pressure of 1.25 atm and a temperature of 298 K when 7.25 g is measured at these conditions?

2. What is the density of oxygen gas at 2.00 atm and 250 K?

3. What is the molar mass of a gas that occupies 4.10 L at a pressure of 1.25 atm and a temperature of 400 K when 12.0 g is measured at these conditions?

4. What is the density of oxygen gas at 800 torr and 300 K?

5. What is the molar mass of a gas when 13.7 g at 250 K and a pressure of 1.0 atm occupies 2.0 L?

Gas stoichiometry

When gases are reacting in a way that is represented by a balanced equation, the stoichiometric relationship of moles to moles is still represented by the coefficients in the balanced equation. The difference is, if the problem starts with the volume of a gas at STP or in the end wants the volume of the gas at STP, the relationship of 1 mol of gas to 22.4 L is used. When the gas is not at STP, the ideal gas equation has to be used to find the number of moles present before the stoichiometry can be done.

Sample Problem 16: Calculate the volume of O_2 needed for 8.9 L of methane to undergo complete combustion at STP.

The balanced equation would be $CH_4(g) + 2O_2(g) \rightarrow CO_2(g) + 2H_2O(g)$.

$$8.9\,L\,CH_4 \times \frac{1\,mol\,CH_4}{22.4\,L} \times \frac{2\,mol\,O_2}{1\,mol\,CH_4} \times \frac{22.4\,L}{1\,mol\,O_2} = x$$

$$x = 18\,L\,O_2$$

Sample Problem 17: If 12.0 L of oxygen gas is produced from the decomposition of hydrogen peroxide at STP, how many moles of hydrogen peroxide decompose?

The equation would be $2H_2O_2(l) \rightarrow O_2(g) + 2H_2O(l)$.

$$12.0\,L\,O_2 \times \frac{1\,mol\,O_2}{22.4\,L} \times \frac{2\,mol\,H_2O_2}{1\,mol\,O_4} = x$$

$$x = 1.07\,mol\,H_2O_2$$

Sample Problem 18: If 1.10 L of oxygen gas at 280 K and 0.98 atm is combined with excess hydrogen gas, how many grams of water vapor will be formed?

The equation is $2H_2(g) + O_2(g) \rightarrow 2H_2O(g)$. First solve $PV = nRT$ to find the moles of O_2.

$$(0.98 \text{ atm})(1.10 \text{ L}) = n(0.0821 \text{ L} \cdot \text{atm} \times K^{-1} \cdot \text{mol}^{-1})(280 \text{ K})$$

$$n = 0.047 \text{ mol}$$

$$0.047 \text{ mol} \times \frac{2 \text{ mol } H_2O}{1 \text{ mol } O_2} \times \frac{18.02 \text{ g } H_2O}{1 \text{ mol } H_2O} = 1.7 \text{ g } H_2O$$

EXERCISE 8·8

Solve the following problems.

1. According to the reaction $CaO(s) + CO_2(g) \rightarrow CaCO_3(s)$, how many liters of carbon dioxide at STP will it take to make 250 g of $CaCO_3$?

2. Ammonia is made in the Haber process, $N_2(g) + 3H_2(g) \rightarrow 2NH_3(g)$ in the presence of a catalyst. How many liters of NH_3 at STP can be made from 95 L of H_2 and an excess of N_2?

3. Mercury can be recovered from mercury(II) oxide according to the reaction $2HgO(s) \rightarrow 2Hg(l) + O_2(g)$. How many grams of Hg are made if 6.75 L of oxygen is collected at STP during this reaction?

4. How many liters of carbon dioxide are given off when 0.800 mol of HCl react with an excess of $NaHCO_3$ at 25°C and 0.95 atm of pressure according to the reaction $NaHCO_3(s) + HCl(aq) \rightarrow NaCl(s) + CO_2(g) + H_2O(l)$?

5. How many grams of carbon dioxide gas will be produced from the combustion of 50.0 g of C_3H_8 at 80°C and 1.10 atm of pressure according to the reaction $C_3H_8(g) + 5O_2(g) \rightarrow 3CO_2(g) + 4H_2O(l)$?

EXERCISE 8·9

Read the following problems and determine which gas law will be necessary to solve for the required quantity.

1. A sample of a gas is cooled from 75.0°C to 50.0°C. If the original volume is 2.00 L, what is the new volume?

2. The pressure of a gas is reduced from 1,160 torr to 760 torr. If the final volume is 450 mL, what is the original volume?

_____

3. A gas has a volume of 0.333 L at 2.25 atm and 201 K. What is its new volume at STP?

_____

4. A 10.0 mL sample of a gas at 1.00 atm is heated from 22.0°C to 100.0°C. If the volume is held constant, what is the new pressure?

_____

5. What is the volume of 148 g of carbon dioxide (CO_2) at STP?

_____

EXERCISE
8·10

Solve each of the problems using the gas law determined in Exercise 8-9.

1. A sample of a gas is cooled from 75.0°C to 50.0°C. If the original volume is 2.00 L, what is the new volume?

_____

2. The pressure of a gas is reduced from 1,160 torr to 760 torr. If the final volume is 450 mL, what is the original volume?

_____

3. A gas has a volume of 0.333 L at 2.25 atm and 201 K. What is its new volume at STP?

_____

4. A 10.0 mL sample of a gas at 1.00 atm is heated from 22.0°C to 100.0°C. If the volume is held constant, what is the new pressure?

_____

5. What is the volume of 148 g of carbon dioxide (CO_2) at STP?

_____

Solutions

9

When one substance dissolves, it is called a *solute*; the substance in which it dissolves is called a *solvent*. Often, but not always, the solvent is simply the substance present in the larger amount. The entire process of a solute dissolving in a solvent is called *solvation*. One characteristic of a solution is that the solute is evenly dispersed within the solvent (so it is called *homogeneous*). The amount of each substance can vary, which is why a solution does not have an exact formula. Many of the solutions you think of are solids dissolved in water—such as saltwater—but there are many other examples, including solutions that are not liquids.

Alloys are examples of solid-solid combinations that do not have an exact formula. This combination is called a solution. Brass is a solution of copper and zinc that have been combined in the molten state and allowed to cool. Another common example is the gas-gas solution in which you live! In the air around you, nitrogen is the solvent and oxygen and carbon dioxide are the main solutes. An example of a liquid-liquid solution is ethanol dissolved in water, and a solution of gas dissolved in water is carbon dioxide dissolved in water. The dissolved carbon dioxide gas in water creates the fizz of sodas!

Can any substance dissolve in any other? No, they must have similar properties to form a solution. This is why oil does not dissolve in water but instead sits on top of it (see Figure 9.1).

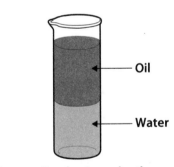

Do not dissolve in each other

Figure 9.1

Chemists will say "like dissolves like" to refer to this effect; since water and oil are not alike, they do not dissolve in each other. There are materials called surfactants that can be added to help substances dissolve in each other that otherwise don't. An example of this is soap (see Figure 9.2). Soap forms a bridge between oil and water, allowing you to clean oils from dishes or your body.

Soap Molecule

Figure 9.2

The unique characteristic of surfactants is that one part of the molecule is "like" the oils nonpolar end but the other half of the molecule is "like" the waters polar end. It is attracted to both molecules! So each soap molecule bridges one water molecule and one oil molecule together.

Two concepts of solutions that we will discuss in this chapter are concentration—which means how much solute is dissolved in a solvent—and limits to solution concentration.

Concentration

There are many ways to express the relative amounts of solute and solvent in a solution. Each one is used in different contexts to make computations easier. Chemists primarily use *molarity*, with the symbol M. Molarity represents how many moles of solute are dissolved compared to the volume in liters of the solution, and is calculated using the formula

$$M = \frac{\text{moles of solute}}{\text{liters of solution}}.$$

Sometimes the amount of solute is provided in grams. This requires knowing the molar mass and the total volume of the solution. All "recipes" for chemical reactions involving solutions will have the concentration expressed as molarity.

Sample Problem 1:   If 50.0 g of NaCl is dissolved in water to make a solution with a volume of 250.0 mL, what is the molarity of the solution?

From the equation, $M = \dfrac{\text{moles of solute}}{\text{liters of solution}}$, we need the moles of NaCl and the volume in liters. From the periodic table, sodium has a molar mass of 22.99 g/mol and chlorine has a molar mass of 35.45 g/mol. The moles of NaCl are found using

$$50.0 \text{ g NaCl} \times \frac{1 \text{ mol NaCl}}{(22.99+35.45)\text{ g NaCl}} = 0.856 \text{ mol NaCl.}$$

To change 250.0 mL to liters, multiply by $\dfrac{1 \text{ L}}{1,000 \text{ mL}}$, which equals 0.2500 L. Substituting into the molarity equation,

$$M = \frac{0.856 \text{ mol NaCl}}{0.2500 \text{ L}} = 3.42 \text{ mol/L.}$$

Sample Problem 2:   If 75.0 g of KNO_3 is dissolved in water to make a solution with a volume of 425 mL, what is the molarity of the solution?

From the equation $M = \dfrac{\text{moles of solute}}{\text{liters of solution}}$, we need moles of KNO_3 and volume in liters. From the periodic table, potassium has a molar mass of 39.10 g/mol, nitrogen has a molar mass of 14.01 g/mol, and oxygen has a molar mass of 16.00 g/mol.

The moles of KNO_3 are

$$75.0\,\text{g KNO}_3 \times \frac{1\,\text{mol KNO}_3}{(39.1+14.01+(3\times16.00))\,\text{g KNO}_3} = 0.742\,\text{mol KNO}_3.$$

Changing milliliters to liters gives

$$425\,\text{mL} \times \frac{1\text{L}}{1{,}000\,\text{mL}} = 0.425\,\text{L}.$$

Substituting into the molarity equation,

$$M = \frac{0.742\,\text{mol KNO}_3}{0.425\,\text{L}} = 1.75\,\text{mol/L}.$$

EXERCISE
9·1

Using the information given and what you have already learned, answer the following questions.

1. Identify the solute(s) and solvent in lemonade.

_____

2. If 250.0 g of calcium sulfate dissolve in enough water to make 500.0 mL of solution, what is the molarity of the solution?

_____

3. How many grams of NaOH are necessary to make 750 mL of 4.25 M solution?

_____

4. If sugar is added to a solution of coffee, what role (or roles) does the coffee play?

_____

5. If 48.0 g of sodium chloride dissolve in 200.0 mL of water, what is the molarity of the resulting solution assuming the solid added does not change the total volume?

_____

6. How many grams of NaOH are necessary to make 250 mL of 1.00 M solution?

_____

7. How many moles of solute is needed to make 1 L of 3.00 M $C_6H_{12}O_6$?

_____

8. How many moles of sodium carbonate, Na_2CO_3, are needed to make 5.00 L of 6.0 M sodium carbonate?

_____

9. How many grams of hydrogen chloride gas is needed to bubble into the solution to make 400.0 mL of 0.100 M solution?

_____

10. If 250.0 g of calcium acetate dissolve in enough water to make 500.0 mL of solution, what is the molarity of the solution?

_____

Diluting a solution

Once a solution of a known molarity is made, it can be used to make other solutions. For aqueous solutions, water will be added. It is important to note that distilled water is best. If tap water—which contains chlorine and dissolved salts—is used, precipitates can form from the reaction with chloride ions or other salts in the water. When a solution is diluted, the starting concentrate is called a stock solution. The stock solution must have a molarity greater than the desired final molarity. The formula to dilute a solution is

$$M_1 V_1 = M_2 V_2,$$

where $M_1 V_1$ refers to the stock solution and $M_2 V_2$ refers to the new solution being made. As before, M is molarity and V is volume. Remember the units of molarity are mol L^{-1}(mol/L), so the volume should be in liters. A problem can ask for the molarity of the stock or the new solution, the volume of the stock solution to use, or the amount of water that needs to be added to dilute the solution.

Sample Problem 3: What is the molarity of a solution using 25.0 mL of 2.00 M of stock solution and adding water to make a volume to 500.0 mL?

First, identify the variables: M_1 = 2.00 M, $V_1 = 25.0\,\text{mL} \times \dfrac{1\,\text{L}}{1,000\,\text{mL}} = 0.0250\,\text{L}$, and $V_2 = 500.0\,\text{mL} \times \dfrac{1\,\text{L}}{1,000\,\text{mL}} = 0.5000\,\text{L}$; M_2 is unknown.

Substituting into the equation $M_1 V_1 = M_2 V_2$:

$$(2.00\text{ M})(0.0250\text{ L}) = (M_2)(0.5000\text{ L})$$

$$M_2 = 0.100\text{ M}$$

Sample Problem 4: How much water should be added to 50.0 mL of a 1.00 M stock solution to make a 0.100 M solution?

First, identify the variables: M_1 = 1.00 M, $V_1 = 50.0\,\text{mL} \times \dfrac{1\,\text{L}}{1,000\,\text{mL}} = 0.0500\,\text{L}$, and M_2 = 0.100 M; V_2 is unknown.

Substituting into the equation $M_1V_1 = M_2V_2$:

$$(1.00\ \text{M})(0.05000\ \text{L}) = (0.100\ \text{M})(V_2)$$

$$V_2 = 0.500\ \text{L} \times \frac{1{,}000\ \text{mL}}{1\ \text{L}} = 500\ \text{mL}$$

If the total volume is 500 mL and 50.0 mL is stock solution, 500 mL − 50.0 mL = 450 mL of water should be added.

Sample Problem 5:   What volume in mL of 3.5 M stock solution should be used to make 100.0 mL of 1.0 M solution?

First, identify the variables: $M_1 = 3.5$ M, $M_2 = 1.0$ M, and $V_2 = 100.0\ \text{mL} \times \dfrac{1\ \text{L}}{1{,}000\ \text{mL}} = 0.1000$ L, V_1 is unknown.

Substituting into the equation $M_1V_1 = M_2V_2$:

$$(3.5\ \text{M})(V_1) = (1.0\ \text{M})(0.1000\ \text{L})$$

$$V_1 = 10.029\ \text{L} \times \frac{1{,}000\ \text{mL}}{1\ \text{L}} = 29\ \text{mL}$$

EXERCISE

9·2

Answer the following questions.

1. What is the molarity of a solution made by diluting 0.25 L of 3.5 M NaCl to 1.0 L?

2. How many liters of 12 M HCl is needed to make 1.0 L of 0.50 M HCl?

3. What is the molarity of a solution made by diluting 400 mL of 8.0 M NaOH to 1.0 L?

4. How many milliliters of 12 M HCl are needed to make 0.50 L of 0.50 M HCl?

5. If 50 mL of 1.0 M NH_4Cl is used, what volume does it need to be diluted to in order to make a 0.25 M solution?

6. What molarity of HNO_3 results if 25 mL of 18 M HNO_3 is diluted to a final volume of 1.0 L?

7. How many mL of 12 M HCl are needed to make 500 mL of 6 M HCl?

8. What is the initial concentration of a solution if 100.0 mL is used to make 1,500.0 mL of 2.0 M solution?

_____

9. How many grams of KNO_3 are dissolved in the solution if diluting it from 0.50 L to 1.0 L gives a new concentration of 0.333 M?

_____

10. You need 250 mL of a 0.100 M solution. You have 50 mL of a 0.500 M stock solution, 75 mL of a 0.250 M stock solution, and as much distilled water as you need. Which stock solution do you use? Why?

_____

Molality

Another way to express concentration is *molality*, with the symbol m. Molality is the ratio of the moles of solute to the mass in kilograms of the solvent; in other words,

$$m = \frac{\text{moles of solute}}{\text{kilograms of solvent}}.$$

If you are given the grams of solute, you need the molar mass of the solute and the mass of the solvent to express the concentration in molarity.

Molality is most often used when determining how a solvent will affect a liquid solution's properties such as boiling point and freezing point. The more solute dissolved, the greater the effect. When a solute is dissolved in a solvent, the boiling point of the solution is higher than the original boiling point. The freezing point of the solution is lower than the original freezing point. This is why in areas where water freezes on the roads as ice, salt is put down to melt the ice, or why salt is added to ice in old-fashioned ice-cream makers. Another common use is to add salt to water in cooking so the water boils at a higher temperature, which cooks the food faster.

Sample Problem 6: What is the molality of a calcium chloride solution made of 47.2 g of $CaCl_2$ and 825 g of water?

First, determine the moles of $CaCl_2$:

$$47.2 \text{ g CaCl}_2 \times \frac{1 \text{ mol CaCl}_2}{(40.08 + (2 \times 35.45)) \text{ g CaCl}_2} = 0.425 \text{ mol CaCl}_2$$

Second, change grams of solvent to kilograms:

$$x \text{ kg} = 825 \text{ g} \times \frac{1 \text{ kg}}{1,000 \text{ g}} \times 0.825 \text{ kg}$$

Third, substitute into the equation:

$$m = \frac{0.425 \text{ mol CaCl}_2}{0.825 \text{ kg}} = 0.515 \text{ mol/kg}$$

Sample Problem 7: Determine the molality of a solution made of 48.8 g of sulfuric acid in 356 g of water.

$$\text{mol H}_2\text{SO}_4 = 48.8 \text{ g H}_2\text{SO}_4 \times \frac{1 \text{ mol H}_2\text{SO}_4}{((1.008 \times 2) + 32.07 + (4 \times 16.00)) \text{ g H}_2\text{SO}_4} = 0.498 \text{ mol H}_2\text{SO}_4$$

$$x \text{ kg} = 356 \text{ g} \times \frac{1 \text{ kg}}{1,000 \text{ g}} = 0.356 \text{ kg}$$

$$m = \frac{0.498 \text{ mol H}_2\text{SO}_4}{0.356 \text{ kg}} = 1.40 \text{ mol/kg}$$

EXERCISE
9·3

Answer the following questions.

1. What is the molality of a solution made by dissolving 4.0 mol of solute in 0.500 kg of solvent?

2. How many moles of solute must be added to 0.250 kg of water to make a 0.100 *m* solution?

3. How many kilograms of solvent are necessary to make 2.00 mol of KI into a 0.50 *m* solution?

4. What is the molality of a solution made with 110 g of NaCl in 0.500 kg of water?

5. How many moles of NH_4Cl must be added to 1.5 kg of water to make a 0.25 *m* solution?

6. How many kilograms of water must be added to 3.00 mol of Na_2CO_3 to make a 2.50 *m* solution?

7. What is the molality of a solution made with 178.6 g of KI in 1,500.0 g of water?

8. How many grams of $CaCl_2$ are necessary to make a 2.45 *m* solution when 0.600 kg of water is used as the solvent?

9. How many kilograms of water are used to make a 0.500 *m* solution of $CaSO_4$ if 125 g of $CaSO_4$ is given as the solute?

10. Which has more solute, 50 mL of 0.50 M NaOH or 0.025 kg of 1.0 *m* NaOH?

Colligative properties

Colligative properties, or *collective properties*, are properties of solutions that depend only on the number of particles of solute present in the solution, regardless of whether those particles are atoms, ions, or molecules. Two such colligative properties are *boiling point* (boiling temperature) and *freezing point* (freezing temperature). Boiling points elevate (go higher) and freezing points depress (go lower) as solute is added to a pure solvent. To know how much a temperature increases or decreases, the amount of particles present in the solution must be known. The equation for boiling-point elevation is

$$\Delta T_b = K_b mi.$$

The equation for freezing-point depression is

$$\Delta T_f = K_f mi.$$

K_f is the freezing-point depression constant and K_b is the boiling-point elevation constant. These values are unique to each solvent.

Looking at the two equations, you will see both have molality (m) being used as the concentration unit. Both equations also have i, which stands for the *van't Hoff factor*—the number of moles of particles in solution per mole of solute.

◆ For most nonelectrolytes in solution, $i = 1$. This is because the solute does not dissociate but remains intact. An example is sugar, which remains as discrete sugar molecules in solution.

   For electrolytes that break into ions, i is the number of ions they form when a formula unit disassociates. NaCl breaks into Na^+ and Cl^-, so $i = 2$.

◆ ΔT is the symbol for temperature change. These equations do not give the new freezing point or boiling point but indicate how much the temperature will change.

   ΔT_b stands for the change in temperature of boiling and ΔT_f stands for the change in temperature of freezing.

◆ The values for the constants needed are determined by experiment and are found in tables. The following table shows some of the constants, which have the unit °C/m.

Solvent	K_f	Normal freezing point	K_b	Normal boiling point
Water (H_2O)	1.86°C/m	0.0°C	0.52°C/m	100.0°C
Benzene (C_6H_6)	5.12°C/m	5.5°C	2.53°C/m	80.1°C

To find the new boiling point and freezing point, the original corresponding temperatures for the pure solvent need to be known. For water solutions at 1 atm of pressure, boiling occurs at 100°C and freezing at 0°C. The ΔT is added to the original boiling point, since it represents an increase— $T_{b\,pure} + \Delta T_{b\,observed} = T_{b\,sol}$ —and is subtracted from the original freezing point, since it means a decrease— $T_{f\,pure} + \Delta T_{f\,observed} = T_{f\,sol}$.

Typical problems ask for the new freezing point or boiling point.

Sample Problem 8:   46.5 g of sodium chloride is added to 500.0 g of water. What are the freezing point and boiling point of the resulting solution?

To determine the molality of the solution, the grams of sodium chloride need to be changed to moles (by dividing by the molar mass) and then divided by the kilograms of solvent.

$$46.5 \text{ g NaCl} \times \frac{1 \text{ mol NaCl}}{58.44 \text{ g NaCl}} = 0.796 \text{ mol NaCl}$$

$$500.0 \text{ g} \times \frac{1 \text{ kg}}{1,000 \text{ g}} = 0.5000 \text{ kg}$$

$$\frac{0.796 \text{ mol}}{0.5000 \text{ kg}} = 1.59 \, m$$

In this case, $i = 2$, since sodium chloride dissociates into Na^+ and Cl^-.

Substituting into $\Delta T_b = K_b m i$,

$$\Delta T_b = \frac{0.52°C}{m} 2(1.59m) = 1.7°C.$$

Substituting into $\Delta T_b + B_p = \text{new } B_p$,

$$1.7°C + 100.0°C = 101.7°C.$$

Substituting into $\Delta T_f = K_f m i$,

$$\Delta T_f = \frac{1.86°C}{m(1.59m)^2} = 5.91°C.$$

Substituting into $F_p - \Delta T_f = \text{new } F_p$,

$$0.00°C - 5.91°C = -5.91°C.$$

**EXERCISE
9·4**

Answer the following questions.

1. What is the new freezing point if 4.0 mol of NaCl is added to 4.0 kg of ice?

_____

2. What is the new boiling point if 0.25 mol of NaCl is added to 2.0 kg of water?

_____

3. How many moles of sugar need to be added to 5.0 kg of water to raise the boiling point by 2.5°C?

_____

4. How many moles of sugar need to be added to 5.0 kg of ice to lower the freezing point by 2.5°C?

_____

5. If the freezing point is lowered by 7.44°C, how many moles of $NaNO_3$ have been added to 5.00 kg of water?

_____

6. If the boiling point is elevated by 5.6°C, how many moles of KCl have been added to 0.250 kg of water?

_____

7. What is the freezing point of a solution that contains 100 g of glucose ($C_6H_{12}O_6$) dissolved completely in 1.00 kg of benzene?

_____

8. What is the boiling point of a solution that contains 5.00 g of ethanol, C_2H_5OH dissolved completely ($i = 1$) in 50.0 g of water?

_____

9. How many grams of Na_2SO_4 must be added to 750 g of water to depress the freezing point of an aqueous solution by 2.5°C?

_____

10. How many grams of NaCl must be added to 2.25 kg of water to raise the boiling point by 0.50°C?

_____

Solubility curves

In most solutions, there is a limit to how much solute will dissolve. The maximum amount of solute that can dissolve in a given amount of solvent depends on temperature. If a graph is made indicating the amount that will dissolve at a given temperature, it is called a solubility curve. The amount dissolved is not always a positive linear relationship. For some substances, such as gases, when the temperature goes up, less gas will dissolve. This explains why sodas go flat when they are open and allowed to reach room temperature or are warmed. For other substances, such as many solids in water, as the temperature increases more solute will dissolve. To know what happens for a particular substance, a solubility curve is needed. Figure 9.3 shows the solubility curves for three substances in water.

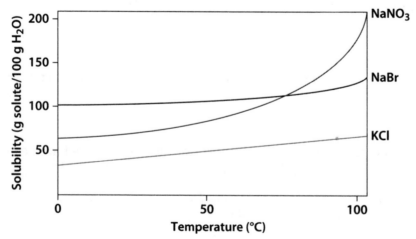

Figure 9.3

The curves show the number of grams of solute that can dissolve for every 100 g of solvent at particular temperatures in degrees Celsius. The concentration unit used here is called *percent*, since it is per 100 g. If the amount dissolved is less than the maximum shown by the curve, the solution is *unsaturated*. If the maximum amount has been dissolved, the solution is *saturated*. If the solution is saturated and more solute is added, the extra solute will not dissolve.

How can you get more solute to dissolve? Change the temperature! For sodium nitrate, only about 60 g will dissolve at 20°C—but if the temperature is increased to 100°C, approximately 180 g will dissolve. How can you do this if water boils at 100°C? Will this solution boil at 100°C? See the discussion on colligative properties for why or why not!

If this solution with the added sodium nitrate at 100°C is then slowly cooled to 20°C without any disturbances, you will have a *supersaturated* solution, since more solute is dissolved at a given temperature than would normally dissolve. If a site is available for a crystal to start to form, the extra 120 g dissolved will come back out of solution as a crystal when the solution is cooled. Supersaturated solutions are what allow you to make rock candy in the kitchen!

EXERCISE
9·5

Use this solubility graph to answer the following questions.

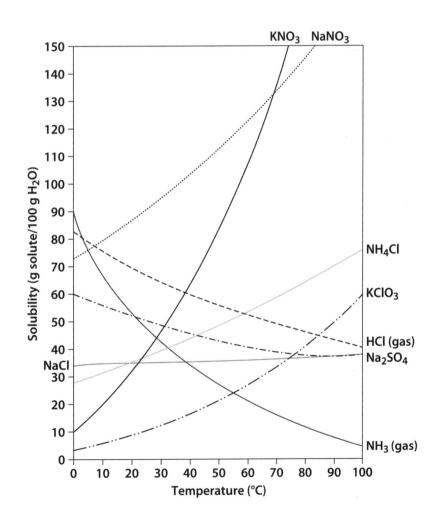

1. Which solid solute has a decreasing solubility as the temperature rises?

_____

2. Which solute has the least change in solubility over the 100°C temperature range?

_____

3. Which solute is most soluble at 0°C?

_____

4. Which solute is most soluble at 30°C?

_____

5. Which solute is most soluble at 70°C?

_____

6. At what temperature do NH_4Cl and Na_2SO_4 have the same solubility?

_____

7. How many grams of HCl will dissolve in 100 g of water at 30°C? Note that here, any excess HCl will be as a gas, not a solid.

_____

8. How many grams of KNO_3 will dissolve in 100 g of water at 70°C?

_____

9. How many grams of $NaNO_3$ will dissolve in 50 g of water at 20°C?

_____

10. How many grams of NaCl will dissolve in 200 g of water at 50°C?

_____

11. At 100°C, is a solution containing 40 g of Na_2SO_4 in 100 g of water saturated, supersaturated, or unsaturated?

_____

12. At 50°C, is a solution containing 60 g of $NaNO_3$ in 100 g of water saturated, supersaturated, or unsaturated?

_____

13. At 20°C, is a solution containing 20 g of $KClO_3$ in 100 g of water saturated, supersaturated, or unsaturated?

_____

14. How many grams of solute will come out of a saturated solution of NH_4Cl when it is rapidly cooled from 80°C to 40°C (assuming that the NH_4Cl was dissolved in 100 g of water)?

_____

Answer the following questions.

1. What is the molarity of a solution made by dissolving 2.50 mol of solute in 2.0 L of water assuming no volume change occurs?

_____

2. What is the molarity of a solution made by dissolving 0.159 mol of solute in 483 mL of water assuming no volume change occurs?

_____

3. What is the molarity of a solution made by dissolving 4.50 g of KNO_3 in enough water to fill a 100.0 mL volumetric flask?

_____

4. What is the molarity of a solution which contains 125 g of KCl in enough water to fill a 500.0 mL volumetric flask?

_____

5. How many grams of NaOH are required to make 2.00 L of 8.0 M NaOH?

_____

6. How many grams of NH_4NO_3 are needed to make 750 mL of a 0.5 M solution?

_____

7. When 20.0 mL of 14.8 M NH_3 is diluted to 250. mL with pure water, what is the concentration of the new solution?

_____

8. How many mL of 6.0 M HCl are needed to make 1.0 L of 3.0 M solution?

_____

9. What is the molality of a solution made by dissolving 0.25 mol of solute in 0.025 kg of solvent?

_____

10. What is the molality of a solution made by dissolving 58.5 g of NaCl in 500 g of water?

_____

11. What is the molality of a solution made by dissolving 1.5 mol of $NaHCO_3$ in 475 mL of water at 25°C? (Hint: you need to use the density of water!)

_____

12. How many moles of solute are needed to make a 3.0 *m* solution that uses 500 g of water?

_____

13. How many grams of water are needed to make a 0.500 m solution that contains 75.0 g of KCl?

_____

14. What is the freezing point of a solution made with 35.0 g of $Al(NO_3)_3$ in 0.250 kg of water?

_____

15. What is the boiling point of the solution made in question 14?

_____

Acids and bases

10

Acid-base theories

When added to water, acids turn litmus paper red and bases turn litmus paper blue. When an acid reacts with a base, water molecules are produced. Why do these things happen? Over a period of time, chemists had several ideas about acids and bases. The first, proposed by Svante Arrhenius, stated that all acids contained H atoms that became H^+ ions in water. Conversely, bases released OH^- ions into water. Pure water itself has equal concentrations of H^+ and OH^-, so the addition of an acid or base upsets the balance of these two ions. The color of the dye litmus depends on which ion was in excess. Water establishes an equilibrium; H^+ ions react with OH^- ions to form water molecules. Water molecules react to form H^+ ions and OH^- ions. The Arrhenius theory explained both phenomena.

There were limitations to this theory. For example, what about ammonia (NH_3), which acts as a base but does not contain the hydroxide ion? Johannes Brønsted and Thomas Lowry proposed instead that acids and bases be identified by their behavior in a reaction. (This is often shortened to just the Brønsted theory.) All acids previously defined by Arrhenius are included correctly, but new ones can be included. A Brønsted acid is a proton (H^+) donor; a Brønsted base is a proton acceptor. A chemical equation can be written to agree with this theory. When ammonia gas is bubbled into water, some ammonium ions and hydroxide ions are formed (Figure 10.1).

$$H_2O(l) + NH_3(g) \rightleftharpoons NH_4^+ + OH^-(aq)$$

Figure 10.1

In this reaction, an H^+ from the water, which has a partial positive charge from the water, interacts with an NH_3 molecule. In this case, water is the proton donor and ammonia is the proton acceptor. By Brønsted's definition, water is behaving as an acid and ammonia is acting as a base. Notice that this reaction has double arrows ($\rightleftharpoons$), indicating that the system will establish an equilibrium, meaning the rate of the forward reaction is equal to the rate of the reverse reaction. This means we also have an acid and base in the reverse reaction!

In the reverse reaction, an H^+ from an NH_4^+ ion is interacting with an OH^- ion, making the ammonium ion a proton donor or acid while the hydroxide ion is a proton acceptor or base (see Figure 10.2).

$$H_2O(l) + NH_3(g) \rightleftharpoons NH_4^+ + OH^-(aq)$$

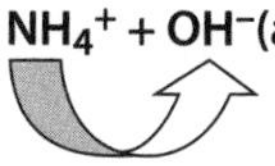

Figure 10.2

Conjugate acid-base pairs

In the reaction being discussed, there are two acids and two bases. This is true for all acid-base reactions! For every acid, once an H^+ is removed, a base remains. These pairs are called conjugate acid-base pairs. In the reaction in Figure 10.3, water is the acid to the hydroxide-ion base. OH^- is the conjugate base of water as an acid.

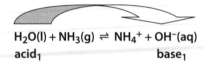

$$H_2O(l) + NH_3(g) \rightleftharpoons NH_4^+ + OH^-(aq)$$
$$\text{acid}_1 \qquad\qquad\qquad \text{base}_1$$

Figure 10.3

The other acid-base pair in the reaction is the ammonia-ammonium ion. Ammonia is acting as a base accepting a proton to make the ammonium-ion conjugate acid. The ammonium ion serves as a conjugate acid in the reverse reaction (see Figure 10.4).

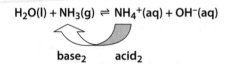

$$H_2O(l) + NH_3(g) \rightleftharpoons NH_4^+(aq) + OH^-(aq)$$
$$\text{base}_2 \quad \text{acid}_2$$

Figure 10.4

Another example of acid-base pairs is water reacting with an acid. The two acid-base pairs in the reaction in Figure 10.5 are (1) hydrochloric acid and the chloride ion conjugate base, and (2) water acting as a base to the hydronium-ion conjugate acid. (Note that a water molecule that has accepted an H^+ to make H_3O^+ is called a hydronium ion.) One difference here is that HCl is a strong acid; it will drive the reaction to the right so that almost all of it forms the product. This will be discussed further later in the chapter. HCl is identified as a strong acid because it transfers almost all of its hydrogen ions to water when in aqueous solution.

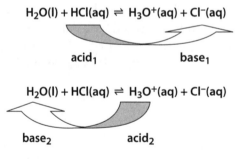

$$H_2O(l) + HCl(aq) \rightleftharpoons H_3O^+(aq) + Cl^-(aq)$$
$$\text{acid}_1 \qquad\qquad \text{base}_1$$

$$H_2O(l) + HCl(aq) \rightleftharpoons H_3O^+(aq) + Cl^-(aq)$$
$$\text{base}_2 \qquad\qquad \text{acid}_2$$

Figure 10.5

EXERCISE
10·1

Identify the acid-base pairs in the following reactions.

1. $H_2O(l) + HNO_3(aq) \rightleftharpoons H_3O^+(aq) + NO_3^-(aq)$ _____

2. $H_2O(l) + SO_4^{2-}(aq) \rightleftharpoons HSO_4^-(aq) + OH^-(aq)$ _____

3. $H_2O(l) + HSO_4^-(aq) \rightleftharpoons OH^-(aq) + H_2SO_4(aq)$ _____

4. $H_2O(l) + HC_2H_3O_2(aq) \rightleftharpoons C_2H_3O_2^-(aq) + H_3O^+(aq)$ _____

5. $H_2S(g) + H_2O(l) \rightleftharpoons HS^-(aq) + H_3O^+(aq)$ _____

6. $HPO_4^{2-}(aq) + H_2O(l) \rightleftharpoons OH^-(aq) + H_2PO_4^-(aq)$ _____

7. $H_2O(l) + HClO_3(aq) \rightleftharpoons H_3O^+(aq) + ClO_3^-(aq)$ _____

8. $HBrO(aq) + H_2O(l) \rightleftharpoons BrO^-(aq) + H_3O^+(aq)$ _____

9. $HCl(aq) + NH_3(aq) \rightarrow NH_4^+(aq) + Cl^-(aq)$ _____

10. $H_2O(l) + HX(aq) \rightarrow H_3O^+(aq) + X^-(aq)$ _____

pH concept

pH is an expression of the concentration in molarity of hydrogen ions, H^+, in solution, and pOH is a measure of the concentration in molarity of hydroxide ions, OH^-, in solution. pH is simply the negative of the logarithm to the base 10 of the molarity of the hydrogen ion concentration. *Traditionally, we discuss only the pH of a solution, since pH and pOH are directly related in a water solution.*

The pH scale is primarily from 0 to 14. In the pH scale, acidic solutions (which have a higher concentration of H^+ than OH^-) range from 0 to 6.9 while basic solutions (which have a higher concentration of OH^- than H^+) range from 7.1 to 14. At 25°C, when the H^+ and OH^- concentrations are the same, 1×10^{-7} M, the negative logarithm—the pH—will be 7. Note: there can be unusual solutions that are extremely acidic with a negative pH (less than 0) and extremely basic solutions with a pH value above 14. A bracket with the substance inside is used to indicate the solution concentration in molarity: $[H^+]$. The following summarizes H^+ and OH^- relationships:

$[H^+] > [OH^-]$: pH is acidic (0–6.9)

$[H^+] = [OH^-]$: pH is neutral (7)

$[H^+] < [OH^-]$: pH is basic (7.1–14)

> Some everyday products that test acidic include orange juice, vinegar, and milk. Some basic products include ammonia; in aqueous solution, Tums and Rolaids (used to neutralize the stomach acid!); caffeine; and milk of magnesia. pH is tested in a variety of ways, including colored dye indicators that are weak acids or bases that change color at different pH values. These can be in the form of paper strips, such as litmus paper, which simply shows if it is acidic or basic (blue paper turns red, indicating an acid, and red paper turns blue, indicating a base); pH paper, which is color sensitive to different pH values and will turn a color you can match to a standard table; or as liquid solutions. pH can also be determined by using pH meters, which use an electrode and circuitry to give a digital display of the pH value.

EXERCISE
10·2

Identify whether each of the following substances is acidic, basic, or neutral based on its pH.

1. Tomatoes   pH = 4.5 _____

2. Baking soda   pH = 8.3 _____

3. Lemon juice   pH = 2.0 _____

4. Milk   pH = 6.6 _____

5. Pure water   pH = 7.0 _____

6. Grapefruit   pH = 3.0 _____

7. Lime—$Ca(OH)_2$ pH = 12.4   _____

8. Human blood   pH = 7.4   _____

9. Acidic buffer   pH = 4.0   _____

10. Basic buffer   pH = 10.0   _____

EXERCISE
10·3

What color will red litmus paper turn in the following substances?

1. Tomatoes   pH = 4.5   _____

2. Baking soda   pH = 8.3   _____

3. Lemon juice   pH = 2.0   _____

4. Milk   pH = 6.6   _____

5. Pure water   pH = 7.0   _____

6. Grapefruit   pH = 3.0   _____

7. Lime—$Ca(OH)_2$ pH = 12.4   _____

8. Human blood   pH = 7.4   _____

9. Acidic buffer   pH = 4.0   _____

10. Basic buffer   pH = 10.0   _____

EXERCISE
10·4

According to the information above, what color will blue litmus paper turn in the following substances?

1. Tomatoes   pH = 4.5   _____

2. Baking soda   pH = 8.3   _____

3. Lemon juice   pH = 2.0   _____

4. Milk   pH = 6.6   _____

5. Pure water   pH = 7.0   _____

6. Grapefruit   pH = 3.0   _____

7. Lime—$Ca(OH)_2$ pH = 12.4   _____

8. Human blood   pH = 7.4   _____

9. Acidic buffer   pH = 4.0   _____

10. Basic buffer   pH = 10.0   _____

Identifying acids

In Chapter 5, when acid naming was presented, acids were identified by names or formulas starting with hydrogen. Some organic acids can also have the hydrogen at the end of the acid formula. This is because when we draw the Lewis structure for an organic acid, traditionally the acidic hydrogen is not at the left but at the right of the molecule drawing.

However, recent practice has changed to write the condensed formula of the acid with the acidic hydrogen on the left just like all other acids. For example, acetic acid in older texts is written CH_3COOH, whereas more recently, following IUPAC recommendations, it is written $HC_2H_3O_2$. IUPAC also recommends a name change from acetic acid to ethanoic acid. Organic acids contain a COOH group, and the IUPAC name will end in the suffix -*oic*, as in ethanoic acid. Remember from the basic organic naming rules that the prefix *eth-* indicates a two-carbon chain. The ethanoic-acid structure is shown in Figure 10.6.

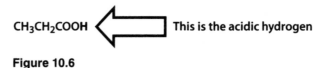
CH_3CH_2COOH This is the acidic hydrogen

Figure 10.6

Other than this simple introduction to organic acids, we are not going to address all the different organic acids.

Chapter 6 explained that even though we write formulas with the ions together in balanced equations, ionic equations show when a substance is extensively ionized in solution. In this section, all reference to "solution" means in water, or "aqueous solution." This is important because acids are identified as strong or weak based on the amount of H^+ that is ionized from the molecule in the solution. Strong acids completely ionize in solution, indicating that in an ionic equation they would be written in their ionic form. The strong acids are listed in Table 10.1.

Table 10.1 Strong Acids

Name	Formula	Ions in solution
Hydrochloric acid	HCl	H^+ and Cl^-
Hydrobromic acid	HBr	H^+ and Br^-
Hydroiodic acid	HI	H^+ and I^-
Perchloric acid	$HClO_4$	H^+ and ClO_4^-
Nitric acid	HNO_3	H^+ and NO_3^-
Sulfuric acid	H_2SO_4	H^+ and HSO_4^- or, if dilute, $2H^+$ and SO_4^{2-}

Note: Only the first hydrogen in H_2SO_4 is considered to be strongly acidic.

Most of the other acids are weak acids. For example, hydrofluoric acid has the formula HF, and in solution it would remain primarily HF, since it does not extensively ionize. It does ionize slightly or it would not test acidic. To compare HCl and HF, in a concentrated solution with 100 molecules of each present, the HCl would split into 100 H^+ and 100 Cl^- ions, while the HF might split into only 3 H^+ and 3 F^- ions, with 97 HF molecules still not ionized in the solution. This small amount of ionization is common in weak acids. HF establishes an equilibrium with water just as other weak acids.

Sample Problem 1: Identify the following acids as weak or strong.

Acetic acid (ethanoic acid), $HC_2H_3O_2$

Hydrochloric acid, HCl

Acetic acid, which is found in vinegar, is a weak acid; hydrochloric acid is strong. Remember, if it is not on the strong list, it is weak.

EXERCISE
10·5

Answer the following questions.

1. Indicate whether substances that test with the pH values listed can be classified as acid, base, or neutral.

   a. pH = 12 _____

   b. pH = 4 _____

   c. pH = 7 _____

   d. pH = 10 _____

   e. pH = 1 _____

   f. pH = 9 _____

   g. pH = 13 _____

   h. pH = 2 _____

   i. pH = 6 _____

   j. pH = 8 _____

2. Indicate whether the following acids are strong or weak.

   a. Hypochlorous acid _____

   b. Hydrobromic acid _____

   c. Nitric acid _____

   d. Nitrous acid _____

   e. Phosphoric acid _____

   f. Oxalic acid _____

   g. Hydrofluoric acid _____

   h. Carbonic acid _____

   i. Hydrochloric acid _____

   j. Phosphorous acid _____

Calculating pH

pH is calculated by taking the negative logarithm of the [H+] concentration. If the pH is known, to find the [H+] concentration, raise 10 to a power equal to the negative value of the pH:

$$pH = -\log[H^+]$$

$$[H^+] = 10^{-pH}$$

pH is calculated on a logarithmic scale in base 10. This means that the difference between the solution concentrations expressed by a pH of 4 and a pH of 5 is not 1, but a factor of 10. The substance with a pH of 4 is 10 times more acidic than the substance with a pH of 5. The difference between a pH of 4 and a pH of 6 is not 2, but a factor of 100. That means that the substance with a pH ions as 100 times as concentrated in hydrogen ions as the substance with the pH of 6!

A short review about logarithms will help you understand how this works. See if you can identify the relationships in the following table:

Number (x)	Number (x) in scientific notation	Log (x)
1	1×10^0	0
10	1×10^1	1
100	1×10^2	2
1,000	1×10^3	3
0.1	1×10^{-1}	−1
0.01	1×10^{-2}	−2
0.001	1×10^{-3}	−3

Notice the exponent in the scientific notation and the log. They are the same, so why does pH use a negative log? The concentration of H+ is usually below 1 M, so the pH scale would all be negative numbers. The negative in the equation makes the numbers come out with positive values.

Sample Problem 2:   Calculate the pH of a 0.015 M solution of HCl.

HCl is a strong acid, hence the concentration of H+ is the concentration of HCl. Substituting into $pH = -\log[H^+]$ gives $pH = -\log[0.015 \text{ M}] = 1.82$.

In logarithmic calculations, the number of significant figures in the answer is equal to the number of significant digits to the right of the decimal point. So the significance of a pH of 1.82 is two digits. The 1 before the decimal point simply establishes the power of 10 represented by the overall value.

Sample Problem 3:   Calculate the pH of a 0.15 M solution of acetic acid that is 1.1% ionized.

Acetic acid is a weak acid, so to find the concentration of H+ ions, change the percentage ionization from 1.1% into a decimal number, 0.011, and multiply it by the concentration of the solution, 0.15 M:

$$0.15 \text{ M} \times 0.011 = 0.0017 \text{ M of } H^+$$

Substituting into $pH = -\log[H^+]$ gives $pH = -\log[0.0017 \text{ M}] = 2.77$.

So even though the concentration of acid is 10 times higher in the acetic acid (0.15 M) than in the previous problem's hydrochloric acid (0.015 M), the solution is not as acidic. Remember, the lower the pH number, the more acidic the solution is; 1.82 is lower than 2.77.

Solve the following problems.

1. What is the pH of a 0.010 M solution of HCl?

2. What is the pH of a 0.25 M solution of HNO_3?

3. What is the pH of a 0.50 M solution of $HClO_4$?

4. What is the pH of a 4.0 M solution of HBr?

5. What is the pH of a 6.0 M solution of H_2SO_4?

6. What is the $[H^+]$ of a solution with a pH of 6.40?

7. What is the $[H^+]$ of a solution with a pH of 11.8?

8. What is the $[H^+]$ of a solution with a pH of 1.50?

9. What is the $[H^+]$ of a solution with a pH of 3.2?

10. What is the $[H^+]$ of a solution with a pH of 9.1?

11. Calculate the pH of a 0.0036 M solution of oxalic acid that is 0.50% ionized.

12. Calculate the pH of a 0.50 M solution of nitrous acid that is 6.2% ionized.

13. Calculate the pH of a 1.0 M solution of acetic acid that is 1.3% ionized.

Identifying bases

Bases are just like acids—in that some are strong and some are weak. Strong bases completely ionize and weak bases only partially ionize, but now the ion involved is hydroxide, OH^-. The strong bases are listed in Table 10.2.

Table 10.2 Strong Bases

Name	Formula	Ions in solution
Lithium hydroxide	LiOH	Li^+ and OH^-
Sodium hydroxide	NaOH	Na^+ and OH^-
Potassium hydroxide	KOH	K^+ and OH^-
Rubidium hydroxide	RbOH	Rb^+ and OH^-
Cesium hydroxide	CsOH	Cs^+ and OH^-
Barium hydroxide	$Ba(OH)_2$	Ba^{2+} and $2OH^-$

If a base is not strong, it is weak. As with acids, when you calculate the pOH for weak bases you need to know the percent ionization.

Sample Problem 4: Identify whether the following bases are weak or strong.

Barium hydroxide

Urea

Barium hydroxide is strong, since it is on the strong list; urea is assumed to be weak, since it is not on the list.

EXERCISE 10·7

Indicate whether the following bases are strong or weak.

1. Aluminum hydroxide _____

2. Sodium hydroxide _____

3. Lithium hydroxide _____

4. Ammonium hydroxide _____

5. Copper(I) hydroxide _____

6. Silver hydroxide _____

7. Rubidium hydroxide _____

8. Diethylamine _____

9. Potassium hydroxide _____

10. Methylamine _____

Calculating pOH

Calculating pOH is the same as calculating pH, except the value of the answer is on the pOH scale.

$$pOH = -log[OH^-]$$

$$[OH^-] = 10^{-pOH}$$

Since chemists traditionally report only pH, how do you change from pOH to pH?

$$pH + pOH = 14$$

Another way to convert to pH is to understand that acid-base solutions contain both acid and base. If pH + pOH equals 14, then using the 10^{-pH} equation and substituting 14 in as 10^{-14}, the answer is 1×10^{-14}. This number represents the concentrations of H^+ and OH^- in pure water at 20°C multiplied together. Therefore, to convert from $[OH^-]$ to $[H^+]$ the following equation is used:

$$[H^+][OH^-] = 1 \times 10^{-14}$$

Sample Problem 5: Calculate the pH of a 0.025 M solution of sodium hydroxide, NaOH.

Sodium hydroxide is a strong base, therefore the concentration of OH^- is 0.025 M. This problem can be solved two ways: using the equation $pOH = -log[OH^-]$ and then the equation $pH + pOH = 14$; or using the equation $[H^+][OH^-] = 1 \times 10^{-14}$ to solve for $[H^+]$ and then using $pH = -log[H^+]$. Both ways are shown.

$$pOH = -log[0.025 \text{ M}] = 1.60$$

$$pH + pOH = 14$$

$$pH + 1.60 = 14$$

$$pH = 12.40 \text{ (very basic)}$$

Or:

$$[H^+][0.025 \text{ M}] = 1 \times 10^{-14}$$

$$[H^+] = 4.0 \times 10^{-13} \text{ M}$$

$$pH = -log[4.0 \times 10^{-13} \text{ M}] = 12.40$$

Sample Problem 6: Calculate the pH of an 0.18 M solution of ammonia, NH_3, which is 2.5% ionized.

Ammonia is a weak base, so the pH is dependent on the percent ionization. Thus, the percent ionization, 2.5%, must be converted to a decimal number and multiplied by the concentration to solve for the pOH. After the pOH is calculated, the pH can be found.

$$0.18 \text{ M} \times 0.025 = 0.0045 \text{ M}$$

$$pOH = -log[0.0045 \text{ M}] = 2.35$$

$$pH + 2.35 = 14.00$$

$$pH = 14.00 - 2.35 = 11.65$$

Solve the following problems.

1. What is the pOH of a solution that has a pH of 3.0?

_____

2. What is the pOH of a solution that has a pH of 7.5?

_____

3. Are the substances in questions 1 and 2 acidic or basic?

_____

4. What is the pOH of a 0.10 M NaOH solution?

_____

5. What is the pH of the solution in question 4?

_____

6. What is the pOH of a 6.0 M NaOH solution?

_____

7. What is the pH of the solution in question 6?

_____

8. What is the [OH⁻] of a solution that has a pOH of 6.0?

_____

9. What is the pH of a 0.25 M solution of a weak base that has been 3.0% ionized?

_____

10. What is the pH of a 1.00 M solution of a weak base that has been 1.10% ionized?

_____

Consolidating all the equations, Figure 10.7 helps us remember what steps to do to change concentrations to pH values.

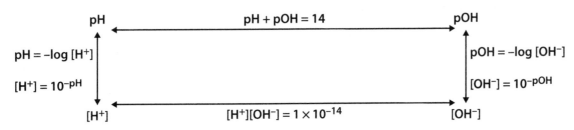

Figure 10.7

Solve the following problems. Be sure to read carefully to know what is given and what is asked for in each question.

1. The pH of a vinegar solution is 2.8; what is its pOH?

_____

2. Calculate the pH and pOH of a solution that contains 0.0085 M [H+].

_____

3. A sample of rainwater has a pH of 6.8; what is its [H+]?

_____

4. Milk of magnesia has a pOH of 3.5; what is its pH?

_____

5. What are the [H+] and [OH−] of a solution whose pH is 9.25?

_____

6. What are the [H+] and [OH−] of a solution whose pOH is 11.45?

_____

7. The juice in strawberries has a pOH of 10.5; what is its pH?

_____

8. Calculate the pH and pOH of a solution that contains 0.75 M [OH−].

_____

9. A sample of a solution of borax has a pH of 9.2; what is its [OH−]?

_____

10. A sample of soft butter has a pOH of 7.9; what is its [OH−]?

_____

_____

Identify the acid-base pairs in the following reactions.

1. $H_2O(l) + HBr(aq) \rightarrow H_3O^+(aq) + Br^-(aq)$ _____

2. $H_2O(l) + C_2H_3O_2^-(aq) \rightarrow HC_2H_3O_2(aq) + OH^-(aq)$ _____

3. $H_2SO_4(aq) + H_2O \rightarrow HSO_4^-(aq) + H_3O^+(aq)$ _____

4. $H_2PO_4^-(aq) + H_3O^+(aq) \rightarrow H_3PO_4(aq) + H_2O(l)$ _____

5. $HPO_4^{2-}(aq) + H_3O^+(aq) \rightarrow H_2PO_4^-(aq) + H_2O(l)$ _____

Identify whether each of the following substances is acidic, basic, or neutral based on its pH.

1. Lye   pH = 13.0 _____

2. Apple juice   pH = 3.0 _____

3. Coffee   pH = 5.0 _____

4. Liquid soap   pH = 10.0 _____

5. Rainwater   pH = 5.6 _____

6. Buffer solution   pH = 5.0 _____

7. Buffer solution   pH = 12.0 _____

8. Buffer solution   pH = 8.0 _____

9. Pure water   pH = 7.0 _____

10. Corn oil   pH = 6.5 _____

Indicate what color each substance will turn each indicator.

	pH	RED LITMUS PAPER	BLUE LITMUS PAPER
1. Lye	13.0	_____	_____
2. Apple juice	3.0	_____	_____
3. Coffee	5.0	_____	_____
4. Liquid soap	10.0	_____	_____
5. Rainwater	5.6	_____	_____
6. Buffer solution	5.0	_____	_____
7. Buffer solution	12.0	_____	_____
8. Buffer solution	8.0	_____	_____
9. Pure water	7.0	_____	_____
10. Corn oil	6.5	_____	_____

Indicate whether each of the following substances is an acid or a base and whether it is strong or weak.

	ACID	BASE	STRONG	WEAK
1. HI(aq)	_____	_____	_____	_____
2. KOH(aq)	_____	_____	_____	_____
3. NH_3(aq)	_____	_____	_____	_____
4. H_2CO_3(aq)	_____	_____	_____	_____
5. HF(aq)	_____	_____	_____	_____
6. HNO_3(aq)	_____	_____	_____	_____
7. LiOH(aq)	_____	_____	_____	_____
8. $Cd(OH)_2$(aq)	_____	_____	_____	_____
9. NH_4OH (aq)	_____	_____	_____	_____
10. H_2SO_3(aq)	_____	_____	_____	_____

Answer the following questions.

1. Calculate the pOH, $[H^+]$, and $[OH^-]$ of a solution with a pH of 8.15.

2. Calculate the pH, $[H^+]$, and $[OH^-]$ of a solution with a pOH of 13.6.

3. Calculate the pH, pOH, and $[H^+]$ of a solution with a $[OH^-] = 4.32 \times 10^{-4}$ M.

4. Calculate the pH, pOH, and $[OH^-]$ of a solution with a $[H^+] = 7.9 \times 10^{-6}$ M.

5. Calculate the pH, pOH, and $[H^+]$ of a solution with an $[OH^-] = 1.00 \times 10^{-7}$ M.

Thermochemistry

11

The study of heat changes in chemical reactions is called *thermochemistry*. Heat is a measure of energy transferred from one system to another. Temperature is the measure of the average kinetic energy of a system. These two should not be confused. Two common units of measure of heat in thermochemistry are the *calorie*, with the symbol cal, and the joule, with the symbol J. Of note is the term *calorie*: this is *not* the calorie unit listed on food labels. The food calorie represents 1,000 calories and is actually a kilocalorie, represented by the symbol cal on food labels. In chemistry we use the kilocalorie, kcal. Temperature is a measure of the hotness or coldness of an object relative to a standard using a temperature scale, which can be Celsius, Fahrenheit, or kelvin.

The calorie is the amount of energy transfer (heat) required to raise the temperature of 1 g of water (at 15°C) by 1°C; it is equivalent to 4.18 J. The conversion factor, then, can be written as either $\dfrac{1\ cal}{4.18\ J}$ or $\dfrac{4.18\ J}{1\ cal}$, depending on the direction of the conversion. Just remember, the unit you want to convert to should be on the top in the ratio of the conversion factor.

Example 1: 385 cal converted to joules

$$385\ cal \times \frac{4.18\ J}{1\ cal} = 1.61 \times 10^{3}\ J$$

Example 2: 987 J converted to calories

$$987\ J \times \frac{1\ cal}{4.18\ J} = 236\ cal$$

Using dimensional analysis along with the previous conversion factors, convert each of the following.

1. 212 J to calories

_____

2. 730 cal to joules

_____

3. 220 J to kilojoules

_____

4. 350 kJ to calories

_____

5. 991 cal to kilojoules

_____

6. 225 kJ to calories

_____

7. 97.0 kcal to joules

_____

8. 35.0 cal to kilocalories

_____

9. 200 cal to joules

_____

10. 150 kJ to calories

_____

Specific heat

Every substance has a different specific heat. That is how much energy must be transferred to raise the temperature of 1.0 g of the substance by 1.0°C. Specific heat is an intensive physical property. On a hot day in the summer, which would you rather slide down—a metal slide or plastic slide? The metal has a low specific heat, which means a small amount of energy will raise its temperature. Also, a metal slide will burn you on the way down because heat will be transferred quickly from the metal to your skin. Plastic has a higher specific heat, so it takes more of the sun's energy to raise its temperature. A high specific heat indicates that it takes more energy to raise a substance's temperature by a certain number of degrees than compared to the same mass of a substance that has a lower specific heat.

If you take an equal number of grams (100.0 g) of aluminum (specific heat of 0.900 J/g°C), water (specific heat of 4.18 J/g°C), and glass (specific heat of 0.753 J/g°C) and give them the same energy (1000.0 J of energy from the sun), which one will be hotter? To solve this we need the equation 11.1 for specific heat, c, where q is the amount of heat, m the mass in grams, and ΔT is the temperature change.

Equation 11.1: $\dfrac{q}{m\Delta T} = c$

which rearranges to

Equation 11.2: $m\Delta T c = q$

$$\Delta T = \dfrac{q}{mc}$$

For aluminum: $\Delta T = 1{,}000.0 \text{ J}/(100.0 \text{ g})(0.900 \text{ J/g°C}) = 11.1\,°C$

For water: $\Delta T = 1{,}000.0 \text{ J}/(100.0 \text{ g})(4.18 \text{ J/g°C}) = 2.39°C$

For glass: $\Delta T = 1{,}000.0 \text{ J}/(100.0 \text{ g})(0.753 \text{ J/g°C}) = 13.2°C$

This also explains why, ideally, you do not want a glass or aluminum coffee cup filled with hot coffee. The aluminum and glass have large changes, meaning that they will absorb large amounts of heat from the beverage and transfer it to your hand.

Table 11.1 lists specific heats to use for the problems in this chapter.

Table 11.1 Specific Heats of Selected Substances

Substance	Specific heat (in J/g°C)
Al	0.900
Au	0.128
CaC_2	1.00
CCl_4	0.856
Cu	0.385
Diamond	0.502
Fe	0.444
Glass	0.753
Graphite	0.720
$H_2O(l)$	4.18
$H_2O(s)$	2.06
$H_2O(g)$	2.02
Pb	0.138
SiO_2	0.749
Sn	0.220
Ti	0.520
Zn	0.390

We can also use Equation 11.1 and rearrange it to solve for specific heat, mass used, or actual initial or final temperature. If solving for a temperature, keep in mind that $\Delta T = T_f$ (temperature final) $- T_i$ (temperature initial)—the *change* in temperature.

Sample Problem 1: What is the final temperature of a 50.0 g piece of aluminum after 350 J of energy is added if the initial temperature is 25.0°C?

Substituting into the equation $\Delta T = \dfrac{q}{mc}$:

$$T_1 f - 25.0°C = 350\ J/(50.0\ g)(0.900\ J/g°C) = 32.8°C$$

Sample Problem 2: How much energy does 500.0 g of water need to absorb to raise its temperature from 25°C to 75°C?

Substituting into $m\Delta Tc = q$:

$$(500.0\ g)(75°C - 25°C)(4.18\ J/g°C) = q$$

$$q = 1.0 \times 10^5\ J\ \text{or}\ 1.0 \times 10^2\ kJ$$

Sample Problem 3: What is the specific heat of a substance whose mass is 45.0 g, initial temperature is 55.0°C, final temperature is 90.0°C, and energy added heat absorbed is 955 J?

Substituting into $\dfrac{q}{m\Delta T} = c$:

$$\frac{955\ J}{(45.0\ g)(90.0°C - 55.0°C)} = c$$

$$c = 0.472 \frac{J}{g}°C$$

EXERCISE

11·2

Answer the following questions. When solving for heat, express your answer in joules.

1. What is the final temperature of 75.0 g of gold that has an initial temperature of 35°C if 750 J of energy is added?

_____

2. How much heat is required to raise 78.5 g of iron from 25.0°C to 80.0°C?

_____

3. How much heat is released when 125 g of water is cooled from 90.0°C to 45.0°C?

_____

4. How much heat is required to raise 8.34 g of silicon dioxide from 17.1°C to 46.7°C?

_____

5. How much heat is released when 49.2 g of graphite is cooled from 75.0°C to 24.1°C?

_____

6. What is the initial temperature if 1.2×10^3 J of energy is added to 35.0 g of copper to reach a final temperature of 95.0°C?

_____

7. What is the final temperature of 50.0 g of aluminum if the initial temperature is 25.0°C and 897 J of energy is added?

_____

8. The temperature of a 477 g sample of water is increased from 18.2°C to 75.8°C. Calculate the amount of heat to cause this change.

_____

9. The temperature of a 6.5 kg sample of copper metal is increased from 18.0°C to 212°C. Calculate the amount of heat to cause this change.

_____

10. Calculate the specific heat of a substance with a mass of 78.4 g, an initial temperature of 62.4°C, a final temperature of 137°C, and 3.6×10^3 J of energy absorbed.

_____

Heat capacity

Heat capacity (C) is an extensive physical property of a substance, meaning it depends on the mass. It represents the amount of energy required to be transferred (heat) to raise the temperature of a given quantity of a substance by 1°C. This means 50.0 g of copper and 75.0 g of copper have different heat capacities. This makes sense, but it means that heat capacities of different substances can't be compared with meaning unless we are comparing similar quantities. That is when specific heat is used. By taking the heat capacity and dividing it by the mass, the specific heat can be calculated:

$$C = mc \quad \frac{C}{m} = c$$

Sample Problem 4: Calculate the specific heat of a piece of chalk with a mass of 10.0 g and a heat capacity of 9.2 J/°C.

$$\frac{\frac{9.2\ \text{J}}{°\text{C}}}{10.0\ \text{g}} = c$$

$$c = 0.92\ \text{J/g°C}$$

Sample Problem 5: Calculate the heat capacity of 78.2 g of copper. Hint: look at Table 11.1.

$$C = (78.2\ \text{g})(0.385\ \text{J/g°C}) = 30.1\ \text{J/°C}$$

EXERCISE
11·3

Answer the following questions.

1. A 43.4 g sample of benzene has a heat capacity of 75.5 J/°C. Calculate the specific heat of benzene.

_____

2. A 2.1 kg sample of steel has a heat capacity of 941 J/°C. Calculate the specific heat of the steel.

_____

3. A 200 g sample of helium in a balloon has a heat capacity of 1.04×10^3 J/°C. Calculate the specific heat of helium.

_____

4. A 151 g sample of hexane has a heat capacity of 341 J/°C. Calculate the specific heat of hexane.

_____

5. A 189 g sample of acetic acid has a heat capacity of 387 J/°C. Calculate the specific heat of acetic acid.

_____

6. Calculate the heat capacity of 358 g of gold.

_____

7. Calculate the heat capacity of a glass window with a mass of 3.1 kg.

_____

8. What is the heat capacity of a 2.50 kg piece of tin metal?

_____

9. What is the heat capacity of a pond of water that has a mass of 225 kg?

_____

10. Calculate the heat capacity of a 345 g sample of carbon tetrachloride.

_____

Calorimetry

Calorimetry is the term applied to measuring changes in temperature as a result of energy transfers. One important application of calorimetry is related to chemical reactions. When chemical reactions take place, energy changes occur as the reaction proceeds. The temperature change in the reaction system and its surroundings are an indication of what energy changes are happening in the reaction. For example, if the surroundings are getting warmer, this is an indication that the reaction system has given off heat. If the surroundings are getting colder, this is an indication that the reaction system has absorbed heat from the surroundings.

When you exercise, your cells give off heat and the surroundings heat up. Cellular metabolism is a chemical reaction. Water (sweat) on your skin absorbs the heat and uses that energy to change from liquid water into water vapor. This process cools you. Reactions or processes that give off heat to warm their surroundings are called exothermic reactions or processes. In exothermic processes a substance cools to the temperature of the surroundings, since it loses the energy it contains by releasing it to the surroundings. Reactions that absorb energy and cool the surroundings are called endothermic reactions processes. The end result in either case is that, when equilibrium is reached, the substance and the surroundings are at the same temperature.

In order to get the best measurements of the temperature change of a reaction, an insulated container must be used. This allows for the minimum amount of heat exchange with the surroundings outside the container. The simplest method is to use a foam coffee cup with a lid placed inside another foam coffee cup; this type of coffee cup is a good insulator (see Figure 11.1). Remember from our discussion of specific heat why, when you drink hot liquids, you would not want to use glass or metal cups: they would burn your hands. They are not good insulators, since they have low specific heats. This type of calorimetry is called constant-pressure calorimetry, since it happens at the prevailing atmospheric pressure, and where the pressure is not changing significantly during the course of the measurements.

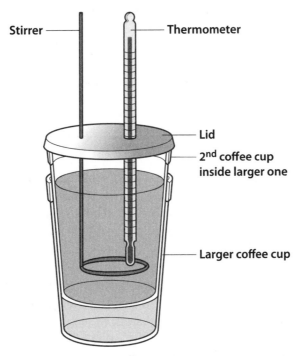

Figure 11.1

Sample Problem 6: If we have 500.0 g of water in a coffee-cup calorimeter heated from 25.0°C to 75.0°C to make hot chocolate, how much energy has been absorbed?

Equation 11.3: $m\Delta Tc = q$,

where m is the mass (in this case of water), ΔT is the temperature change, c is the specific heat, and q is the heat released or absorbed. This is the same equation as equation 11.2—a calorimeter follows the same rules.

$$(500.0 \text{ g})(75.0°C - 25.0°C)(4.18 \text{ J/g°C}) = q$$

$$q = 1.05 \times 10^5 \text{ J or } 105 \text{ kJ}$$

EXERCISE
11·4

Solve the following problems.

1. What is the final temperature in a constant-pressure calorimeter that contains 525 g of water and has an initial temperature of 5.0°C before 8,710 J of energy is added?

2. How many joules of energy must be added to 625 g of water to cause a 51.0°C change in temperature in a constant-pressure calorimeter?

_____

3. When 9,250 J of energy is added to 341 g of water in a constant-pressure calorimeter, by how many degrees does the temperature of the water change?

_____

4. What is the initial temperature of water in a constant-pressure calorimeter containing 156 g of water if 2.5 kJ of energy is added and the final temperature is 97.0°C?

_____

5. Calculate the final temperature in a constant-pressure calorimeter containing 500.0 g of water after 87.5 kJ of energy is added if the initial temperature is 17.0°C.

_____

If you put a hot substance into contact with a cold substance, the system will adjust until both substances are at the same temperature. The energy is transferred from the warmer substance to the cooler one, by the vibrations of the atoms of molecules. This does not mean the temperature will be exactly halfway between the two temperatures! That works if you mix the same quantities of the same substance or if the combination of masses and specific heats cancel out. A piece of metal at 90°C dropped into water at 20°C might equalize at 25°C! This is due to differences in specific heats. To solve this type of problem, the key is applying the Law of Conservation of Energy. Energy cannot be created or destroyed, so that the energy lost by the warmer substance ($-q$) will equal the energy gained by the cooler substance ($+q$). The quantities of heat lost equals the heat gained, just the signs are opposite. Since the value of the qs are equal, we can place the two specific-heat equations together using $q_2 + q_1 = 0$:

Equation 11.4: $(m_1 \Delta T_1 c_1) + (m_2 \Delta T_2 c_2) = 0$,

where ΔT is defined as $T_{final} - T_{initial}$ and T. The subscript 1 refers to one of the substances and the subscript 2 to the other.

Sample Problem 7: If a 10.0 g piece of gold at 87.00°C is placed in 155 g of water at 25.00°C, what will be the final temperature of the system (assuming no losses to the surroundings, i.e., in a good constant pressure calorimeter)?

Setting up the temperature on each side requires you to think about the system. The final temperature is going to be between the two extremes. ΔT can be positive or negative, depending on whether the substance is getting warmer or getting colder.

Using equation 11.4, and gold as substance 1 and water as substance 2, $m_1 = 10.00$ g, $\Delta T_1 = T_f - 87.00°C$, $c_1 = 0.128$ J/g°C, $m_2 = 155$ g, $\Delta T_2 = T_f - 25.00°C$, and $c_2 = 4.18$ J/g°C. Specific heats are from Table 11.1.

$$[(10.0 \text{ g})(T_f - 87.00°\text{C})(0.128 \text{ J/g}°\text{C})] + [(155 \text{ g})(T_f - 25.00°\text{C})(4.18 \text{ J/g}°\text{C})] = 0$$

$$T_f = 25.12°\text{C}$$

Not much of a temperature change for the water (0.12°C) but a large one for the gold (61.88°C). For any other types of problems, determine each variable and substitute into the equation accordingly.

Sample Problem 8: Calculate the number of grams of water in a constant-pressure calorimeter if a 25.0 g piece of aluminum at 75.0°C is dropped into water at 30.0°C and the final temperature of the system is 31.5°C. The specific heats are taken from Table 11.1.

Using the aluminum as substance 1 and water as substance 2, $m_1 = 25.0$ g, $\Delta T_1 = 31.5°C - 75.0°C$, $c_1 = 0.900$ J/g°C, $\Delta T_2 = 31.5°C - 30.0°C$, and $c_2 = 4.18$ J/g°C; m_2 is unknown.

$$[(25.0\,g)(31.5°C - 75.0°C)(0.900\,J/g°C)] + [(xg)(31.5°C - 30.0°C)(4.18\,J/g°C)] = 0$$
$$m_2 = 156\,g$$

Answer the following questions. Assume all reactions take place in a constant-pressure calorimeter with negligible heat capacity.

1. A piece of lead with a mass of 18.9 g at a temperature of 93.4°C is dropped into 165 g of water at an initial temperature of 18.0°C. What is the final temperature of the system?

2. If a piece of gold with a mass of 15.18 g and a temperature of 145°C is dropped into 250.0 g of water at 15.4°C, what is the final temperature of the system?

3. A sample of water at 27.2°C has a 67.1 g sample of iron added to it at 97.0°C. What amount of water is present if the final temperature of the system is 30.0°C?

4. A piece of unknown insoluble compound with a mass of 19.1 g is heated to 99.8°C and dropped into 28.0 g of water at 20.0°C. If the final temperature of the system is 28.7°C, what is the specific heat and the identity of the compound?

5. If a piece of zinc with a mass of 37.45 g and a temperature of 105°C is dropped into 250.0 g of water at 25.4°C, what will be the final temperature of the system?

6. What is the final temperature of a system when 125 g of SiO_2 at 89.5°C is placed in 200.0 g of water at 5.00°C?

7. A piece of unknown metal with a mass of 39.1 g is heated to 89.7°C and dropped into 158.0 g of water at 20.0°C. If the final temperature of the system is 22.1°C, what are the specific heat and the identity of the metal?

8. A piece of iron with a mass of 57.9 g at a temperature of 99.4°C is dropped into 465 g of water at an initial temperature of 8.00°C. What is the final temperature of the system?

9. A sample of water at 37.70°C has a 55.1 g sample of zinc added to it at 87.0°C. What amount of water is present if the final temperature of the system is 40.00°C?

10. A piece of glass with a mass of 18.9 g at a temperature of 83.4°C is dropped into 105 g of water at an initial temperature of 28.0°C. What is the final temperature of the system?

In all these problems, the calorimeter was of negligible heat capacity. Unfortunately, even the best-insulated calorimeters do absorb some of the energy. This means that to fully calculate the energy absorbed in the reaction, it is necessary to know how much energy the calorimeter itself has absorbed. This is the heat capacity of the calorimeter, with units of J/°C.

The temperature change multiplied by the heat capacity gives the amount of energy absorbed by the calorimeter. The total heat is therefore equal to the heat absorbed by the calorimeter plus heat calculated. (Another type of calorimeter we will not look into here is the constant-volume bomb calorimeter.)

Sample Problem 9: A reaction is carried out in a constant-pressure calorimeter with a heat capacity of 2.3 J/°C. If the temperature of the system increases by 5.8°C, how much energy is absorbed by the calorimeter?

$$q = (2.3 \text{ J/°C})(5.8°C) = 13 \text{ J}$$

Sample Problem 10: In a system that had 551 J of energy absorbed by the system and 18 J absorbed by the calorimeter, what is the total amount of energy given off by the reaction?

$$q = 551 \text{ J} + 18 \text{ J} = 569 \text{ J}$$

EXERCISE
11·6

Answer the following questions. Each question is about a different reaction.

1. A reaction occurs in a constant-pressure calorimeter with a heat capacity of 1.6 J/°C. If the temperature of the system increased by 15.9°C, how much energy is absorbed by the calorimeter?

2. A reaction occurs in a constant-pressure calorimeter with a heat capacity of 0.13 kJ/°C. If the temperature of the system increases by 45.8°C, how much energy does the calorimeter absorb? Be careful with units.

3. If the amount of heat absorbed by the water in a calorimeter is 480 J and the calorimeter absorbs 25 J, what is the total energy given off by a reaction occuring in the water?

4. If the amount of heat absorbed by the water in a calorimeter is 921 J and the calorimeter has a heat capacity of 2.71 J/°C, what is the total energy given off by a reaction in the water if the temperature increases by 72.0°C?

_____

5. If the amount of heat absorbed by the water is 1,158 J and the calorimeter has a heat capacity of 5.79 J/°C, what is the total energy given off by a reaction in the water if the temperature increased by 77.0°C?

_____

EXERCISE
11·7

Review earlier parts of this chapter by solving the following problems. Be sure to carefully read both the given and desired units. For questions 6 through 15, practice algebraic manipulation by rearranging the given equation as indicated to solve for the designated parameter.

1. How many joules are in 3,500 cal?

_____

2. How many calories are in 575 J?

_____

3. If you have 1.00 kJ, how many calories do you have?

_____

4. A certain candy bar has 230 cal. How many joules is this?

_____

5. A reaction gives off 3,520 kJ of energy. How many calories is this?

_____

6. Solve $q = mc\Delta T$ for m.

_____

7. Solve $q = mc\Delta T$ for c.

_____

8. Solve $q = mc\Delta T$ for ΔT.

_____

9. Solve $q = mc\Delta T$ for T_f.

_____

10. Solve $q = mc\Delta T$ for T_i.

_____

11. Solve $C = mc$ for m.

_____

12. Solve $C = mc$ for c.

_____

13. Solve $(m_1 \Delta T_1 c_1) + (m_2 \Delta T_2 c_2) = 0$ for T_f.

_____

14. Solve $(m_1 \Delta T_1 c_1) + (m_2 \Delta T_2 c_2) = 0$ for m_1.

_____

15. Solve $(m_1 \Delta T_1 c_1) + (m_2 \Delta T_2 c_2) = 0$ for c_1 and explain how to find the identity of substance 1.

_____

Answer key

1   Matter: classification, properties, and changes

1·1   1. Homogeneous mixture   2. Element   3. Compound   4. Heterogeneous mixture   5. Heterogeneous mixture   6. Homogeneous mixture   7. Element   8. Compound   9. Heterogeneous mixture   10. Element   11. Homogeneous mixture   12. Compound   13. Element   14. Heterogeneous mixture   15. Compound

1·2   1. Physical   2. Physical   3. Chemical   4. Physical   5. Chemical   6. Physical   7. Physical   8. Chemical   9. Physical   10. Physical   11. Intensive   12. Extensive   13. Intensive   14. Extensive   15. Intensive   16. Extensive   17. Intensive   18. Intensive   19. Intensive   20. Intensive

1·3   1. Chemical   2. Physical   3. Chemical   4. Physical   5. Chemical   6. Physical   7. Physical   8. Physical   9. Physical   10. Chemical   11. Physical   12. Chemical   13. Chemical   14. Physical   15. Physical

1·4   1. The density of the ring is $23.46 \text{ g}/2.25 \text{ cm}^3 = 10.4 \text{ g/cm}^3$. Since gold's density is 19.3 g/cm^3, the ring is not made of pure gold.   2. Metal 1: $55.33 \text{ g}/7.75 \text{ cm}^3 = 7.14 \text{ g/cm}^3$—the metal is zinc. Metal 2: $61.5 \text{ g}/4.52 \text{ cm}^3 = 13.6 \text{ g/cm}^3$—the metal is mercury. Metal 3: $19.4 \text{ g}/2.45 \text{ cm}^3 = 7.92 \text{ g/cm}^3$—the metal is probably iron.   3. 28.6 mL   4. 133 g   5. 11 g/cm^3 6. 2.70 g/cm^3 7. 1.189 g/mL   8. The density of this wood is 1.75 kg/dm^3 or 1.75 g/cm^3. It will sink in water, as its density is greater than the density of water.   9. 193 g   10. 2.34 cm^3

1·5   1. 0.77 g/mL   2. Ethanol

3.

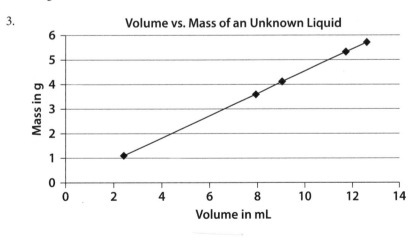

4. 0.455 g/mL   5. This substance will float on the ethanol in questions 1 and 2 if it does not dissolve in it first.

1·6   1. Homogeneous mixture   2. Element   3. Heterogeneous mixture   4. Compound   5. Heterogeneous mixture

1·7 1. Physical, intensive   2. Physical, extensive   3. Chemical, intensive   4. Physical, intensive   5. Chemical, intensive   6. Physical, intensive

1·8 1. Both   2. Physical   3. Chemical   4. Chemical   5. Physical   6. Physical   7. Physical   8. Both   9. Both   10. Both

1·9 1. 21.2 g; gold   2. 0.790 g/mL; acetone   3. 0.48 cm^3; 2.2 g/cm^3 4. 35 g; 7.9 g/cm^3 5. 38 mL; hexane

2   Measurement, mathematical notations, and conversions

2·1 1. 7.5×10^2 g   2. 9.4632×10^4 mL   3. 1.0×10^{-2} kg   4. 5.8×10^{-3} L   5. 2.00×10^5 mg   6. 8.020×10^2 g   7. 5.0500×10^3 mL   8. 2.20×10^2 mL   9. 1.01×10^{-3} g   10. 2×10^{-3} g   11. 0.00051 cm   12. 2,800 g   13. 521.01 mL   14. 0.0000633 km   15. 4,600 g   16. 0.0004 cm^3 17. 160.0 g   18. 2,834,000 g   19. 0.0003240 mL   20. 0.2705 g

2·2 1. 42.6 mL   2. 33.9 mL   3. 26.0 mL   4. 16.2 mL   5. 10.0 mL

2·3 1. 98.0 mL   2. 41.5 mL   3. 16.5 mL   4. 9.40 mL

2·4 1. 2   2. 3   3. 1   4. 3   5. 3   6. 4   7. 1   8. 2   9. 4   10. 6   11. 3   12. 2   13. 3   14. 4   15. 4   16. 4   17. 2   18. 3   19. 5   20. 1

2·5 1. 6.3 m   2. 842 mL   3. 37 cm   4. 810 mg   5. 14 m^2 6. 33.4 cm   7. 0.80 kg/m^3 8. 0.9 (units cancel)   9. 31 cm   10. 0.2 m/s   11. 1.51 g/mL   12. 193 cm^2 13. 13 dm^2 14. 200 m   15. 10.2 cm   16. 16 m^2 17. 3 L   18. 28 g   19. 30 g/cm^3 20. 152 g

2·6 1. Student 2's measurements were more accurate—they came closer to the true value of 43.7 mL. Student 2's measurements were also more precise than student 1's, as the range in student 2's measurements from the actual value was only ±0.2 mL, versus student 1's range of ±1.5 mL from the actual value.   2. Precise   3. Accurate and precise

2·7

1. $\dfrac{100_0 \text{ g}}{1 \text{ kg}}$

2. $\dfrac{1{,}000 \text{ ml}}{1 \text{ L}}$

3. $\dfrac{1 \text{ m}}{100 \text{ cm}}$

4. $\dfrac{1 \text{ min}}{60 \text{ s}}$

5. $\dfrac{1 \text{ km}}{1{,}000 \text{ m}}$ and $\dfrac{3{,}600 \text{ s}}{1 \text{ hr}}$ or $\dfrac{60 \text{ s}}{1 \text{ min}}$ and $\dfrac{60 \text{ min}}{1 \text{ hr}}$

6. $\dfrac{1{,}000 \text{ g}}{1 \text{ kg}}$ and $\dfrac{1{,}000 \text{ mg}}{1 \text{ g}}$ or $\dfrac{1 \times 10^6 \text{ mg}}{1 \text{ kg}}$

7. $\dfrac{1 \text{ m}}{1 \times 10^9 \text{ nm}}$ and $\dfrac{1 \text{ km}}{1{,}000 \text{ m}}$ or $\dfrac{1 \text{ km}}{1 \times 10^{12} \text{ nm}}$

8. $\dfrac{1{,}000 \text{ g}}{1 \text{ kg}}$

9. $\dfrac{1 \text{ m}}{100 \text{ cm}}$ and $\dfrac{1 \text{ km}}{1{,}000 \text{ m}}$ or $\dfrac{1 \text{ km}}{1 \times 10^5 \text{ cm}}$

10. $\dfrac{24 \text{ hr}}{1 \text{ day}}$, $\dfrac{60 \text{ min}}{1 \text{ hr}}$ and $\dfrac{60 \text{ s}}{1 \text{ min}}$ or $\dfrac{24 \text{ hr}}{1 \text{ day}}$ and $\dfrac{3,600 \text{ s}}{1 \text{ hr}}$

2·8   1. 2,500 g   2. 783 mL   3. 0.914 m   4. 0.10 m/s   5. 3.05 km/h   6. 750,000 mg or 7.5×10^5 mg
7. 0.0000000015 km or 1.5×10^{-9} km   8. 520 g   9. 0.00065 km or 6.5×10^{-4} km   10. 86,400 seconds

2·9   1. 87 g   2. 18 mL   3. 44.3 mL   4. 29 g   5. 2.5 cm³

2·10   1. 4.56×10^2 m   2. 8.6×10^{-3} kg   3. 1×10^7 μL   4. 2×10^3 cm   5. 7.5×10^{-9} Tbytes

2·11   1. 1   2. 3   3. 4

2·12   1. 46.7 g; 45.6 g has two sig figs, 0.234 g has three sig figs, and 0.87 g has two sig figs   2. 1,803 mL; 1,808 mL has four sig figs and 5.00 mL has three sig figs   3. 5×10^{-6} km² or 0.000005 km²; 0.00685 km has three sig figs and 0.0007 km has one sig fig   4. 260 m/s; 9,040,000 m has three sig figs and 35,000 s has two sig figs   5. 2.3 g/mL; 5.36 g has three sig figs, 4.5 mL has two sig figs, and 2.2 mL has two sig figs

2·13

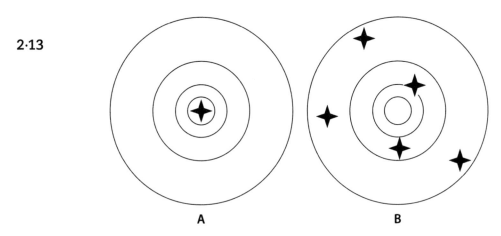

A   B

2·14   1. 86,400 s   2. 5.0×10^{-7} L   3. 5×10^{12} nm   4. 33 m/s   5. 4.86×10^{-6} g/mL

3   Atomic structure and nuclear reactions

3·1   1. 31; 15; 15; 16; 15   2. 60; 27; 27; 33; 27   3. Carbon-14; 6; 8   4. ^{37}Cl⁻; 37; 17   5. 43; 20; 23; 20
6. Plutonium-242; 242; 94   7. Chromium-50; 24; 26   8. ^{65}Cu²⁺; 29; 36   9. 15; 7; 7; 8; 7
10. 34; 16; 16; 18; 18

3·2   1. $^{31}_{15}$P   2. $^{60}_{27}$Co   3. $^{14}_{6}$C   4. $^{37}_{17}$Cl¹⁻   5. $^{211}_{82}$Pb   6. $^{46}_{22}$Ti   7. $^{222}_{86}$Rn   8. $^{25}_{12}$Mg
9. $^{191}_{77}$Ir   10. $^{22}_{10}$Ne

3·3   1. 24 amu   2. 80. amu   3. 195 amu   4. 192 amu   5. 52 amu

3·4   1. $^{241}_{95}$Am   2. $^{4}_{2}$He or $^{4}_{2}\alpha$ 3. $^{237}_{93}$Np   4. $^{0}_{-1}\beta$ or $^{0}_{-1}e^-$ 5. $^{229}_{90}$Th   6. $^{4}_{2}$He or $^{4}_{2}\alpha$ 7. $^{225}_{89}$Ac
8. $^{225}_{89}$Ac   9. $^{217}_{85}$At   10. $^{217}_{85}$At   11. $^{213}_{83}$Bi   12. $^{209}_{82}$Pb   13. $^{209}_{83}$Bi

3·5   1. 6.25%   2. 16 g   3. 14.4 y   4. 8,000 y   5. 12 min   6. 16 days   7. 4.09×10^{11} atoms   8. 7 days
9. 6.16×10^{15} atoms   10. 4.93×10^9 atoms

3·6   1. Millikan   2. Thomson   3. Rutherford   4. Thomson   5. Thomson   6. Rutherford   7. Bohr
8. Chadwick

3·7   1. p⁺; positive; 1; in the nucleus   2. Electron; negative; 0; outside the nucleus
3. Neutron; n⁰; 1; in the nucleus

3·8   1. Alpha particle   2. β and gamma ray   3. Alpha particle   4. β and gamma ray   5. Gamma ray
6. Alpha particle   7. Alpha particle   8. Gamma ray   9. β   10. β and gamma ray

3·9   1. $_{-1}^{0}\beta$ or $_{-1}^{0}e^-$ 2. $_{36}^{76}\mathrm{Kr}$ 3. $_{0}^{1}\mathrm{n}$ 4. $_{54}^{146}\mathrm{Xe}$ 5. $_{10}^{22}\mathrm{Ne}$ 6. $_{86}^{198}\mathrm{Rn} \rightarrow {}_{2}^{4}\mathrm{He} + {}_{84}^{184}\mathrm{Po}$ 7. $_{78}^{199}\mathrm{Pt} \rightarrow {}_{79}^{139}\mathrm{Au} + {}_{-1}^{0}\beta$

8. $_{77}^{174}\mathrm{Ir} \rightarrow {}_{2}^{4}\mathrm{He} + {}_{75}^{194}\mathrm{Re}$ 9. $_{106}^{263}\mathrm{Sg} \rightarrow {}_{2}^{4}\mathrm{He} + {}_{104}^{259}\mathrm{Rf}$ 10. $_{79}^{211}\mathrm{Au} \rightarrow {}_{80}^{211}\mathrm{Hg} + {}_{-1}^{0}\beta$

4   The periodic table, periodicity, and periodic trends

4·1   1. Nonmetal; gas; 16; 2;   2. Metalloid; solid; 14; 3   3. Metal; liquid; 12; 6   4. Barium; metal; solid
5. Neon; nonmetal; gas   6. Bromine; nonmetal; liquid   7. Metal; solid; 1; 7   8. Nonmetal; gas; 18; 6
9. Metalloid; solid; 14; 4

4·2   1. $1s^2 2s^2 2p^2$

2. $1s^2 2s^2 2p^6 3s^2 3p^6 4s^2 3d^{10}$

3. $1s^2 2s^2 2p^6 3s^2 3p^6 4s^2 3d^{10} 4p^5$

4. $1s^2 2s^2 2p^6 3s^2 3p^6 4s^2 3d^{10} 4p^6 5s^2 4d^{10} 5p^6 6s^1$

5. $1s^2 2s^2 2p^6 3s^2 3p^6 4s^2 3d^{10} 4p^6 5s^2 4d^{10} 5p^6 6s^2 4f^{14} 5d^{10} 6p^3$

6. $1s^2 2s^2 2p^6 3s^2 3p^6 4s^1$

7. $1s^2 2s^2 2p^6 3s^2 3p^6 4s^2 3d^5$

8. $1s^2 2s^2 2p^6 3s^2 3p^6 4s^2 3d^{10} 4p^6 5s^2 4d^{10} 5p^5$

9. $1s^2 2s^2 2p^6 3s^2 3p^6 4s^2 3d^{10} 4p^6 5s^2 4d^{10}$

10. $1s^2 2s^2 2p^6 3s^2 3p^6 4s^2 3d^{10} 4p^6 5s^2 4d^{10} 5p^6 6s^2 4f^{14} 5d^{10} 6p^2$

11. $1s^2 2s^2 2p^6 3s^2 3p^6 4s^2 3d^{10} 4p^6 5s^2 4d^{10} 5p^6 6s^2 4f^{14} 5d^{10} 6p^6 7s^1$

12. $1s^2 2s^2 2p^6 3s^2 3p^6 4s^2 3d^{10} 4p^6 5s^2 4d^{10} 5p^6 6s^2 4f^{14} 5d^8$

13. $1s^2 2s^2 2p^6 3s^2 3p^6 4s^2 3d^2$

14. $1s^2 2s^2 2p^4$

15. $1s^2 2s^2$

4·3   1. $1s^2 2s^1$ and $1s^2$

2. $1s^2 2s^2 2p^6 3s^2 3p^1$ and $1s^2 2s^2 2p^6$

3. $1s^2 2s^2 2p^6 3s^2 3p^6 4s^2 3d^{10} 4p^6 5s^2 4d^{10} 5p^6 6s^2 4f^{14} 5d^{10} 6p^2$ and $1s^2 2s^2 2p^6 3s^2 3p^6 4s^2 3d^{10} 4p^6 5s^2 4d^{10} 5p^6 4f^{14} 5d^{10}$

4. $1s^2 2s^2 2p^3$ and $1s^2 2s^2 2p^6$

5. $1s^2 2s^2 2p^6 3s^2 3p^5$ and $1s^2 2s^2 2p^6 3s^2 3p^6$

6. $1s^2 2s^2 2p^4$ and $1s^2 2s^2 2p^6$

7. $1s^2 2s^2 2p^6 3s^1$ and $1s^2 2s^2 2p^6$ 8. $1s^2 2s^2 2p^6 3s^2 3p^6 4s^2 3d^{10} 4p^3$ and $1s^2 2s^2 2p^6 3s^2 3p^6 3d^{10}$

9. $1s^2 2s^2 2p^5$ and $1s^2 2s^2 2p^6$

10. $1s^2 2s^2$ and $1s^2$

11. $1s^2 2s^2 2p^6 3s^2 3p^6 4s^2 3d^{10} 4p^3$ and $1s^2 2s^2 2p^6 3s^2 3p^6 4s^2 3d^{10} 4p^6$

12. $1s^2 2s^2 2p^6 3s^2 3p^6 4s^2 3d^8$ and $1s^2 2s^2 2p^6 3s^2 3p^6 3d^8$

13. $1s^2 2s^2 2p^6 3s^2 3p^6 4s^2 3d^{10} 4p^6 5s^2 4d^{10}$ and $1s^2 2s^2 2p^6 3s^2 3p^6 4s^2 3d^{10} 4p^6 4d^{10}$

14. $1s^2 2s^2 2p^6 3s^2 3p^6 4s^2 3d^{10} 4p^6 5s^2$ and $1s^2 2s^2 2p^6 3s^2 3p^6 4s^2 3d^{10} 4p^6$

15. $1s^2 2s^2 2p^6 3s^2 3p^6 4s^2 3d^6$ and $1s^2 2s^2 2p^6 3s^2 3p^6 3d^5$

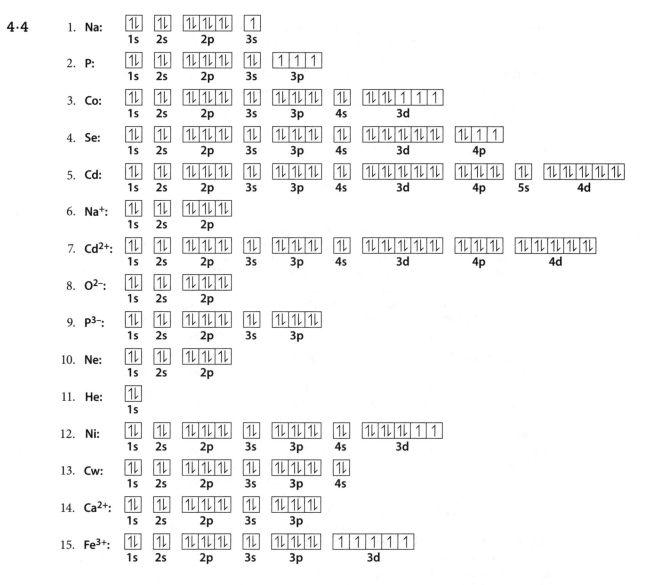

4·4

1. **Na:** 1s ↑↓ | 2s ↑↓ | 2p ↑↓ ↑↓ ↑↓ | 3s ↑

2. **P:** 1s ↑↓ | 2s ↑↓ | 2p ↑↓ ↑↓ ↑↓ | 3s ↑↓ | 3p ↑ ↑ ↑

3. **Co:** 1s ↑↓ | 2s ↑↓ | 2p ↑↓ ↑↓ ↑↓ | 3s ↑↓ | 3p ↑↓ ↑↓ ↑↓ | 4s ↑↓ | 3d ↑↓ ↑↓ ↑ ↑ ↑

4. **Se:** 1s ↑↓ | 2s ↑↓ | 2p ↑↓ ↑↓ ↑↓ | 3s ↑↓ | 3p ↑↓ ↑↓ ↑↓ | 4s ↑↓ | 3d ↑↓ ↑↓ ↑↓ ↑↓ ↑↓ | 4p ↑↓ ↑ ↑

5. **Cd:** 1s ↑↓ | 2s ↑↓ | 2p ↑↓ ↑↓ ↑↓ | 3s ↑↓ | 3p ↑↓ ↑↓ ↑↓ | 4s ↑↓ | 3d ↑↓ ↑↓ ↑↓ ↑↓ ↑↓ | 4p ↑↓ ↑↓ ↑↓ | 5s ↑↓ | 4d ↑↓ ↑↓ ↑↓ ↑↓ ↑↓

6. **Na⁺:** 1s ↑↓ | 2s ↑↓ | 2p ↑↓ ↑↓ ↑↓

7. **Cd²⁺:** 1s ↑↓ | 2s ↑↓ | 2p ↑↓ ↑↓ ↑↓ | 3s ↑↓ | 3p ↑↓ ↑↓ ↑↓ | 4s ↑↓ | 3d ↑↓ ↑↓ ↑↓ ↑↓ ↑↓ | 4p ↑↓ ↑↓ ↑↓ | 4d ↑↓ ↑↓ ↑↓ ↑↓ ↑↓

8. **O²⁻:** 1s ↑↓ | 2s ↑↓ | 2p ↑↓ ↑↓ ↑↓

9. **P³⁻:** 1s ↑↓ | 2s ↑↓ | 2p ↑↓ ↑↓ ↑↓ | 3s ↑↓ | 3p ↑↓ ↑↓ ↑↓

10. **Ne:** 1s ↑↓ | 2s ↑↓ | 2p ↑↓ ↑↓ ↑↓

11. **He:** 1s ↑↓

12. **Ni:** 1s ↑↓ | 2s ↑↓ | 2p ↑↓ ↑↓ ↑↓ | 3s ↑↓ | 3p ↑↓ ↑↓ ↑↓ | 4s ↑↓ | 3d ↑↓ ↑↓ ↑↓ ↑ ↑

13. **Cw:** 1s ↑↓ | 2s ↑↓ | 2p ↑↓ ↑↓ ↑↓ | 3s ↑↓ | 3p ↑↓ ↑↓ ↑↓ | 4s ↑↓

14. **Ca²⁺:** 1s ↑↓ | 2s ↑↓ | 2p ↑↓ ↑↓ ↑↓ | 3s ↑↓ | 3p ↑↓ ↑↓ ↑↓

15. **Fe³⁺:** 1s ↑↓ | 2s ↑↓ | 2p ↑↓ ↑↓ ↑↓ | 3s ↑↓ | 3p ↑↓ ↑↓ ↑↓ | 3d ↑ ↑ ↑ ↑ ↑

4·5 1. Oxygen has the smaller radius because it has eight protons in its nucleus compared to seven protons in nitrogen's nucleus. This additional proton increases the effective nuclear charge, making oxygen's radius smaller.   2. Potassium has the smaller radius because it has electrons in only four energy levels versus rubidium's five energy levels.   3. Chlorine has the smallest radius. Bromine has electrons in four energy levels, while sulfur and chlorine have electrons in only three energy levels; thus sulfur and chlorine have atomic radii smaller than bromine's. Chlorine's atomic radius is smaller than sulfur's because chlorine has 17 protons in its nucleus versus the 16 protons in sulfur's nucleus, resulting in a greater effective nuclear charge for chlorine.   4. Strontium has the smallest radius, since it has electrons in only five energy levels, whereas cesium and barium both have electrons in six energy levels.   5. Krypton has the smaller atomic radius because it has electrons in one less energy level than rubidium.   6. Gallium has a smaller atomic radius than calcium because it has a larger effective nuclear charge due to its having one more proton pulling in on the same number of energy levels.   7. Fluorine has a smaller atomic radius than iodine because fluorine has three fewer energy levels of electrons surrounding its nucleus than iodine.   8. Fluorine has the smaller atomic radius because it has a greater effective nuclear charge than boron.   9. Nitrogen and carbon both have smaller atomic radii than silicon, since they have electrons spread over one less energy level than silicon; nitrogen has the smallest atomic radius of the three because it has a greater effective nuclear charge than carbon.   10. Neon has the smallest atomic radius because it has electrons spread over the smallest number of energy levels.

4·6 1. Configurations: $1s^22s^22p^5$ and $1s^22s^22p^6$; ratios: 9:9 and 9:10. The F^- ion has the larger radius, since it has gained an electron, thus reducing the effective nuclear charge. 2. Configurations: $1s^22s^22p^63s^23p^1$ and $1s^22s^22p^6$; ratios: 13:13 and 13:10. The aluminum atom has the larger radius, since the cation has lost electrons, thus increasing its effective nuclear charge. 3. Configurations: $1s^22s^22p^63s^23p^64s^23d^6$ and $1s^22s^22p^63s^23p^63d^6$; ratios: 26:26 and 26:24. The iron atom has the larger radius for the same reason as the aluminum atom—the cation has lost electrons, thus increasing its effective nuclear charge. 4. Configurations: $1s^22s^22p^63s^23p^64s^23d^{10}4p^3$ and $1s^22s^22p^63s^23p^64s^23d^{10}4p^6$; ratios: 33:33 and 33:36. The As^{3-} ion has the larger radius for the same reason as the F^- anion—it has gained electrons, thus reducing its effective nuclear charge. 5. Configurations: $1s^22s^22p^3$ and $1s^22s^22p^6$; ratios: 7:7 and 7:10. The N^{3-} ion has the larger radius for the same reason as the F^- anion—it has gained electrons, thus reducing its effective nuclear charge. 6. Configurations: $1s^22s^22p^4$ and $1s^22s^22p^6$; ratios: 8:8 and 8:10. The O^{2-} ion has the larger radius for the same reason as the F^- anion—it has gained electrons, thus reducing its effective nuclear charge. 7. Configurations: Na $1s^22s^22p^63s^1$ and $1s^22s^22p^6$; ratios: 11:11 and 11:10. The sodium atom has the larger radius for the same reason as the aluminum atom—the cation has lost electrons, thus increasing its effective nuclear charge. 8. Configurations: $1s^22s^22p^63s^23p^64s^23d^{10}4p^1$ and $1s^22s^22p^63s^23p^64s^23d^{10}$; ratios: 33:33 and 33:30. The gallium atom has the larger radius, since the cation has lost electrons, thus increasing its effective nuclear charge. 9. Configurations: Cr $1s^22s^22p^63s^23p^64s^23d^4$ and $1s^22s^22p^63s^23p^6$; ratios: 24:24 and 24:18. The chromium atom has the larger radius for the same reason as the aluminum atom—the cation has lost electrons, thus increasing its effective nuclear charge. 10. Configurations: $1s^22s^22p^63s^2$ and $1s^22s^22p^6$; ratios: 12:12 and 12:10. The magnesium atom has the larger radius for the same reason as the aluminum atom—the cation has lost electrons, thus increasing its effective nuclear charge.

4·7 1. Carbon has the smaller first ionization energy, since it has less effective nuclear charge. 2. Rubidium has the smaller first ionization energy, since it has more shielding across five energy levels than potassium's four energy levels. 3. Selenium and bromine have smaller first ionization energies than sulfur because they experience more shielding, due to having four energy levels compared to sulfur's three. Selenium has the smallest first ionization energy of the three, since its nucleus has one less proton than bromine's, and thus less effective nuclear charge. 4. Francium has the smallest first ionization energy, since it has the most shielding between its nucleus and the outermost electrons: it has seven energy levels compared to rubidium's five and cesium's six. 5. Aluminum has the smaller first ionization energy, since it is easier to remove a single electron from the 3p cloud than to remove an electron from the filled 3s cloud. 6. Francium has the smaller first ionization energy, since it has more shielding than oxygen, due to many more energy levels of electrons between the nucleus and the outermost electrons. 7. Without measuring, we are unable to determine which atom has the smaller first ionization energy. Chlorine has a smaller first ionization energy than fluorine (same group, different effective nuclear charge), but nitrogen also has a smaller first ionization energy than fluorine (same period, different amount of shielding). 8. Neon has the smaller first ionization energy, since it has more shielding than helium, due to its having one more energy level of electrons between the nucleus and the outermost electrons. 9. Gallium has the smaller first ionization energy, since it has more shielding than boron, due to its having two more energy levels of electrons between the nucleus and the outermost electrons. 10. Silver has the smaller first ionization energy, since it has more shielding than copper, due to its having one more energy level of electrons between the nucleus and the outermost electrons.

4·8 1. Nonmetal; liquid; 17; 4 2. Metalloid; solid; 15; 5 3. Metal; solid; 4; 4 4. Tin; metal; solid 5. Fluorine; nonmetal; gas 6. Hydrogen; nonmetal; gas

4·9 1. $1s^22s^22p^63s^23p^64s^23d^{10}4p^6$

2. $1s^22s^22p^63s^23p^64s^23d^5$

3. $1s^22s^22p^4$

4. $1s^22s^22p^63s^23p^64s^23d^{10}4p^65s^24d^{10}5p^66s^2$

5. $1s^22s^22p^63s^23p^64s^23d^{10}4p^65s^24d^{10}5p^5$

4·10 1. $1s^22s^22p^63s^23p^64s^23d^{10}4p^65s^24d^{10}$ and $1s^22s^22p^63s^23p^64s^23d^{10}4p^64d^{10}$

2. $1s^22s^22p^63s^23p^64s^23d^{10}4p^4$ and $1s^22s^22p^63s^23p^64s^23d^{10}4p^6$

4·11

1. **Be:** $\boxed{\uparrow\downarrow}$ $\boxed{\uparrow\downarrow}$
   1s 2s

2. **F:** $\boxed{\uparrow\downarrow}$ $\boxed{\uparrow\downarrow}$ $\boxed{\uparrow\downarrow}\boxed{\uparrow\downarrow}\boxed{\uparrow}$
   1s 2s 2p

3. **K:** $\boxed{\uparrow\downarrow}$ $\boxed{\uparrow\downarrow}$ $\boxed{\uparrow\downarrow}\boxed{\uparrow\downarrow}\boxed{\uparrow\downarrow}$ $\boxed{\uparrow\downarrow}$ $\boxed{\uparrow\downarrow}\boxed{\uparrow\downarrow}\boxed{\uparrow\downarrow}$ $\boxed{\uparrow}$
   1s 2s 2p 3s 3p 4s

4·12

1. K; same; K; K   2. Same; Cl; Na; Na   3. K; K^+; K; K   4. Same; Br; Br^-; Br

5 Naming compounds and writing formulas

5·1
1. K_2O 2. $SrCl_2$ 3. AlN 4. Li_3P 5. $Al(ClO_3)_3$ 6. $Be_3(PO_3)_2$ 7. $CaSO_4$ 8. $NaNO_3$
9. $Al_2(C_2O_4)_3$ 10. $(NH_4)_2SO_4$ 11. $NaNO_2$ 12. KNO_3 13. Al_2S_3 14. FeO 15. Fe_2O_3
16. $Pb(C_2H_3O_2)_2$ 17. $Ga(ClO_3)_3$ 18. $(NH_4)_2S$ 19. Ag_2O 20. MnO_2

5·2
1. Aluminum sulfide 2. Potassium phosphate 3. Copper(II) sulfate 4. Zinc nitrate 5. Iron(II) carbonate 6. Tin(II) hypobromite 7. Lead(IV) chloride 8. Manganese(IV) oxide 9. Calcium permanganate 10. Cesium oxide 11. Silver bromide 12. Chromium(III) chloride 13. Potassium carbonate 14. Iron(II) sulfide 15. Aluminum hydroxide 16. Cadmium sulfide 17. Iron(III) chloride 18. Calcium phosphate 19. Nickel(II) nitrate 20. Lead(II) oxide

5·3
1. CO_2 2. SO_3 3. H_2O 4. P_4O_{10} 5. S_2Cl_2 6. SiF_4 7. N_2O_4 8. NO_2 9. Cl_2O_7
10. CS_2

5·4
1. Dinitrogen pentoxide 2. Carbon tetrabromide 3. Diphosphorus trioxide 4. Phosphorus trichloride 5. Silicon dioxide 6. Boron trifluoride 7. Nitrogen monoxide 8. Sulfur hexafluoride 9. Chlorine dioxide 10. Carbon monoxide

5·5
1. $HBrO_3$ 2. HIO_4 3. HI 4. HF 5. $HMnO_4$ 6. H_2SO_3 7. H_2CO_3 8. HNO_3
9. $HC_2H_3O_2$ 10. H_3PO_4

5·6
1. Hydroiodic acid 2. Phosphoric acid 3. Carbonic acid 4. Fluorous acid 5. Bromous acid 6. Hydrochloric acid 7. Oxalic acid 8. Hydrofluoric acid 9. Nitrous acid 10. Sulfurous acid

5·7
1. C_3H_8 2. C_8H_{18} 3. C_5H_{12} 4. $C_{10}H_{22}$ 5. C_9H_{20} 6. C_6H_{14} 7. C_7H_{16} 8. CH_4 9. C_2H_6
10. C_4H_{10}

5·8
1. Nonane 2. Hexane 3. Heptane 4. Since the number of hydrogen atoms does not equal $2n + 2$, this compound cannot be named based on the system presented in this book. 5. Methane 6. Ethane 7. Propane 8. Butane 9. Octane 10. Decane

5·9
1. M-NM 2. M-NM 3. NM-NM 4. M-NM 5. NM-NM 6. A 7. NM-NM 8. M-NM 9. M-NM 10. A 11. M-NM 12. M-NM 13. NM-NM 14. M-NM 15. M-NM

5·10
1. L 2. I 3. O; carbon disulfide 4. K 5. M 6. O; hydroiodic acid 7. H 8. O; potassium fluoride 9. O; aluminum hypochlorite 10. O; sulfuric acid 11. N 12. E 13. F 14. B 15. O; sodium bromide

5·11
1. D 2. J 3. B 4. G 5. F 6. A 7. I 8. H 9. E 10. C

6 Chemical reactions

6·1
1. Skeleton equation: $BaCl_2(aq) + Na_2CO_3(aq) \rightarrow NaCl(aq) + BaCO_3(s)$; balanced equation: $BaCl_2(aq) + Na_2CO_3(aq) \rightarrow 2NaCl(aq) + BaCO_3(s)$

2. Skeleton equation: $KOH(aq) + FeCl_3(aq) \rightarrow Fe(OH)_3(s) + KCl(aq)$; balanced equation: $3KOH(aq) + FeCl_3(aq) \rightarrow Fe(OH)_3(s) + 3KCl(aq)$

3. Skeleton equation: $Cu(s) + AgNO_3(aq) \rightarrow Ag(s) + Cu(NO_3)_2(aq)$; balanced equation: $Cu(s) + 2AgNO_3(aq) \rightarrow 2Ag(s) + Cu(NO_3)_2(aq)$

4. Skeleton equation: $Cl_2(g) + KBr(aq) \rightarrow Br_2(l) + KCl(aq)$; balanced equation: $Cl_2(g) + 2KBr(aq) \rightarrow Br_2(l) + 2KCl(aq)$

5. Skeleton equation: $BaCl_2(aq) + ZnSO_4(aq) \rightarrow ZnCl_2(aq) + BaSO_4(s)$; balanced equation: $BaCl_2(aq) + ZnSO_4(aq) \rightarrow ZnCl_2(aq) + BaSO_4(s)$

6. Skeleton equation: $Al(NO_3)_3(aq) + NaOH(aq) \rightarrow NaNO_3(aq) + Al(OH)_3(s)$; balanced equation: $Al(NO_3)_3(aq) + 3NaOH(aq) \rightarrow 3NaNO_3(aq) + Al(OH)_3(s)$

7. Skeleton equation: $Al(s) + CuCl_2(aq) \rightarrow AlCl_3(aq) + Cu(s)$; balanced equation: $2Al(s) + 3CuCl_2(aq) \rightarrow 2AlCl_3(aq) + 3Cu(s)$

8. Skeleton equation: $BaCl_2(aq) + Na_2SO_4(aq) \rightarrow NaCl(aq) + BaSO_4(s)$; balanced equation: $BaCl_2(aq) + Na_2SO_4(aq) \rightarrow 2NaCl(aq) + BaSO_4(s)$

9. Skeleton equation: $SO_3(s) \rightarrow SO_2(g) + O_2(g)$; balanced equation: $2SO_3(s) \rightarrow 2SO_2(g) + O_2(g)$

10. Skeleton equation: $Cl_2(g) + LiI(aq) \rightarrow LiCl(aq) + I_2(s)$; balanced equation: $Cl_2(g) + 2LiI(aq) \rightarrow 2LiCl(aq) + I_2(s)$

6·2

1. Product: $Fe_2O_3(s)$; balanced equation: $4Fe(s) + 3O_2(g) \rightarrow 2Fe_2O_3(s)$

2. Product: $Mg_3N_2(s)$; balanced equation: $3Mg(s) + N_2(g) \rightarrow Mg_3N_2(s)$

3. Product: $H_2SO_4(aq)$; balanced equation: $SO_3(g) + H_2O(l) \rightarrow H_2SO_4(aq)$

4. Product: $CaO(s)$; balanced equation: $2Ca(s) + O_2(g) \rightarrow 2CaO(s)$

5. Product: $HCl(g)$; balanced equation: $H_2(g) + Cl_2(g) \rightarrow 2HCl(g)$

6. Product: $NaCl(s)$; balanced equation: $2Na(s) + Cl_2(g) \rightarrow 2NaCl(g)$

7. Product: $NaOH(aq)$; balanced equation: $Na_2O(s) + H_2O \rightarrow 2NaOH(aq)$

8. Product: $Fe_2O_3(s)$; balanced equation: $4Fe(s) + 3O_2(g) \rightarrow 2Fe_2O_3(s)$

9. Product: $HNO_2(aq)$; balanced equation: $N_2O_3(g) + H_2O(g) \rightarrow 2HNO_2(aq)$

10. Product: $Al_2O_3(s)$; balanced equation: $4Al(s) + 3O_2(g) \rightarrow 2Al_2O_3(s)$

6·3

1. Products: $H_2(g)$ and $O_2(g)$; balanced equation: $2H_2O(l) \rightarrow 2H_2(g) + O_2(g)$

2. Products: $KCl(s)$ and $O_2(g)$; balanced equation: $2KClO_3(s) \rightarrow 2KCl(s) + 3O_2(g)$

3. Products: $Hg(l)$ and $O_2(g)$; balanced equation: $2HgO \rightarrow 2Hg(l) + O_2(g)$

4. Products: $CO_2(g)$ and $H_2O(l)$; balanced equation: $H_2CO_3(aq) \rightarrow CO_2(g)$ and $H_2O(l)$

5. Products: $CaO(s)$ and $H_2O(l)$, or $Ca(s)$ and $H_2O(l)$; balanced equation: $Ca(OH)_2(aq) \rightarrow CaO(s) + H_2O(l)$ or $Ca(OH)_2(aq) \rightarrow Ca(s) + 2H_2O(l)$

6. Products: $Li_2O(s)$ and $CO_2(g)$; balanced equation: $Li_2CO_3(s) \rightarrow Li_2O(s) + CO_2(g)$

7. Products: $NaCl(s)$ and $O_2(g)$; balanced equation: $2NaClO_3(s) \rightarrow 2NaCl(s) + 3O_2(g)$

8. Products: $Na(s)$ and $Cl_2(g)$; balanced equation: $2NaCl(l) \rightarrow 2Na(s) + Cl_2(g)$

9. Products: $Ag(s)$ and $O_2(g)$; balanced equation: $2Ag_2O(s) \rightarrow 4Ag(s) + O_2(g)$

10. Products: $H_2O(l)$ and $SO_2(g)$; balanced equation: $H_2SO_3(aq) \rightarrow H_2O(l) + SO_2(g)$

6·4

1. Products: $Li_2O(s)$ and $H_2(g)$; balanced equation: $2Li(s) + H_2O(l) \rightarrow Li_2O(s) + H_2(g)$

2. Products: $KF(aq)$ and $I_2(s)$; balanced equation: $F_2(g) + 2KI(aq) \rightarrow 2KF(aq) + I_2(s)$

3. Products: $Zn(OH)_2(s)$ and $H_2(g)$; balanced equation: $Zn(s) + 2H_2O(g) \rightarrow Zn(OH)_2(s) + H_2(g)$

4. Products: $PbSO_4(s)$ and $H_2(g)$; balanced equation: $H_2SO_4(aq) + Pb(s) \rightarrow PbSO_4(s) + H_2(g)$

5. Products: $ZnCl_2(aq)$ and $H_2(g)$; balanced equation: $Zn(s) + 2HCl(aq) \rightarrow ZnCl_2(aq) + H_2(g)$

6. Products: $Br_2(l)$ and $KCl(aq)$; balanced equation: $Cl_2(g) + 2KBr(aq) \rightarrow Br_2(l)$ and $2KCl(aq)$

7. Products: $KOH(aq)$ and $H_2(g)$; balanced equation: $2K(s) + 2H_2O(l) \rightarrow 2KOH(aq) + H_2(g)$

8. Products: $Ag(s)$ and $Cu(NO_3)_2(aq)$; balanced equation: $Cu(s) + 2AgNO_3(aq) \rightarrow 2Ag(s) + Cu(NO_3)_2(aq)$

9. Products: $NaF(aq)$ and $Cl_2(g)$; balanced equation: $F_2(g) + 2NaCl(aq) \rightarrow 2NaF(aq) + Cl_2(g)$

10. Products: $Cu(s)$ and $Fe(NO_3)_3(aq)$; balanced equation: $2Fe(s) + 3Cu(NO_3)_2(aq) \rightarrow 3Cu(s) + 2Fe(NO_3)_3(aq)$

6·5

1. Products: $NH_4I(aq)$ and $AgNO_3(s)$; balanced equation: $NH_4I(aq) + AgNO_3(aq) \rightarrow NH_4NO_3(aq) + AgI(s)$

2. Products: $NaNO_3(aq)$ and $PbSO_4(s)$; balanced equation: $Na_2SO_4(aq) + Pb(NO_3)_2(aq) \rightarrow 2NaNO_3(aq) + PbSO_4(s)$

3. Products: $Cu(OH)_2(s)$ and $KCl(aq)$; balanced equation: $CuCl_2(aq) + 2KOH(aq) \rightarrow Cu(OH)_2(s) + 2KCl(aq)$

4. Products: $AlPO_4$(s) and $NaNO_3$(aq); balanced equation: $Al(NO_3)_3$(aq) + Na_3PO_4(aq) → $AlPO_4$(s) + $3NaNO_3$(aq)

5. Products: $NaNO_3$(aq) and $PbCl_2$(s); balanced equation: $2NaCl$(aq) + $Pb(NO_3)_2$(aq) → $2NaNO_3$(aq) + $PbCl_2$(s)

6. Products: NH_4NO_3(aq) and $Fe(OH)_2$(s); balanced equation: $2NH_4OH$(aq) + $Fe(NO_3)_2$(aq) → $2NH_4NO_3$(aq) + $Fe(OH)_2$(s)

7. Products: $BaSO_4$(s) and $KClO_3$(aq); balanced equation: $Ba(ClO_3)_2$(aq) + K_2SO_4(aq) → $BaSO_4$(s) + $2KClO_3$(aq)

8. Products: $LiCl$(aq) and $Mg(OH)_2$(s); balanced equation: $2LiOH$(aq) + $MgCl_2$(aq) → $2LiCl$(aq) + $Mg(OH)_2$(s)

9. Products: $SrSO_4$(s) and $NiBr_2$(aq); balanced equation: $SrBr_2$(aq) + $NiSO_4$(aq) → $SrSO_4$(s) + $NiBr_2$(aq)

10. Products: $Zn(OH)_2$(s) and KI(aq); balanced equation: ZnI_2(aq) + $2KOH$(aq) → $Zn(OH)_2$(s) + $2KI$

6·6

1. $2C_4H_{10}$(g) + $13O_2$(g) → $8CO_2$(g) + $10H_2O$(g)   2. C_7H_{16}(g) + $11O_2$(g) → $7CO_2$(g) + $8H_2O$(g)

3. $2C_{10}H_{22}$(g) + $31O_2$(g) → $20CO_2$(g) + $22H_2O$(g)   4. $2C_8H_{18}$(g) + $25O_2$(g) → $16CO_2$(g) + $18H_2O$(g)

5. $2C_2H_6$(g) + $7O_2$(g) → $4CO_2$(g) + $6H_2O$(g)

6·7

1. Products: NiI_3(aq) and H_2O(l); balanced equation: $Ni(OH)_3$(s) + $3HI$(aq) → NiI_3(aq) + $3H_2O$(l)

2. Products: K_2SO_4(aq) and H_2O(l); balanced equation: H_2SO_4(aq) + $2KOH$(aq) → K_2SO_4(aq) + $2H_2O$(l)

3. Products: $Ca(NO_3)_2$(aq) and H_2O(l); balanced equation: $Ca(OH)_2$(aq) + $2HNO_3$(aq) → $Ca(NO_3)_2$(aq) + $2H_2O$(l)

4. Products: Na_2SO_4(aq) and H_2O(l); balanced equation: H_2SO_4(aq) + $2NaOH$(aq) → Na_2SO_4(aq) + $2H_2O$(l)

5. Products: and KF(aq) and H_2O(l); balanced equation: HF(aq) + KOH(aq) → KF(aq) + H_2O(l)

6. Products: Li_3PO_4(s) and H_2O(l); balanced equation: H_3PO_4(aq) + $3LiOH$(aq) → Li_3PO_4(s) + $3H_2O$(l)

7. Products: $CaCl_2$(aq) and H_2O(l); balanced equation: $Ca(OH)_2$ (aq) + $2HCl$(aq) → $CaCl_2$(aq) + $2H_2O$(l)

8. Products: $Mg_3(PO_4)_2$(s) and H_2O(l); balanced equation: $3Mg(OH)_2$ (aq) + $2H_3PO_4$(aq) → $Mg_3(PO_4)_2$(s) + $6H_2O$(l)

9. Products: $BaCl_2$(aq), H_2O(l), and CO_2(g) (Note: the carbonic acid decomposes to water and carbon dioxide gas); balanced equation: $BaCO_3$(s) + $2HCl$(aq) → $BaCl_2$(aq) + H_2O(l) + CO_2(g)

10. Products: K_2SO_4(aq) and H_2O(l); balanced equation: H_2SO_4(aq) + $2KOH$(aq) → K_2SO_4(aq) + $2H_2O$(l)

6·8

1. Ionic equation: Na^+(aq) + PO_4^{3-}(aq) + Ag^+(aq) + NO_3^-(aq) → Na^+(aq) + NO_3^-(aq) + Ag_3PO_4(s); net ionic equation: PO_4^{3-}(aq) + Ag^+(aq) → Ag_3PO_4(s); balanced net ionic equation: PO_4^{3-}(aq) + $3Ag^+$(aq) → Ag_3PO_4(s)

2. Ionic equation: K^+(aq) + OH^-(aq) + Sr^{2+}(aq) + Cl^-(aq) → K^+(aq) + Cl^-(aq) + $Sr(OH)_2$(s); net ionic equation: OH^-(aq) + Sr^{2+}(aq) → $Sr(OH)_2$(s); balanced net ionic equation: $2OH^-$(aq) + Sr^{2+}(aq) → $Sr(OH)_2$(s)

3. Ionic equation: Br_2(l) + K^+(aq) + I^-(aq) → K^+(aq) + Br^-(aq) + I_2(s); net ionic equation: Br_2(l) + I^-(aq) → Br^-(aq) + I_2(s); balanced net ionic equation: Br_2(l) + $2I^-$(aq) → $2Br^-$(aq) + I_2(s)

4. Ionic equation: H^+(aq) + Cl^-(aq) + K^+(aq) + OH^-(aq) → H_2O(l) + K^+(aq) + Cl^-(aq); net ionic equation: H^+(aq) + OH^-(aq) → H_2O(l); balanced net ionic equation: H^+(aq) + OH^-(aq) → H_2O(l)

5. Ionic equation: NH_4^+(aq) + S^{2-}(aq) + Ag^+(aq) + $C_2H_3O_2^-$(aq) → NH_4^+(aq) + $C_2H_3O_2^-$(aq) + Ag_2S(s); net ionic equation: S^{2-}(aq) + Ag^+(aq) → Ag_2S(s); balanced net ionic equation: S^{2-}(aq) + $2Ag^+$(aq) → Ag_2S(s)

6. Ionic equation: Cl_2(g) + Li^+(aq) + Br^-(aq) → Li^+(aq) + Cl^-(aq) + Br_2(l); net ionic equation: Cl_2(g) + Br^-(aq) → Cl^-(aq) + Br_2(l); balanced net ionic equation: Cl_2(g) + $2Br^-$(aq) → $2Cl^-$(aq) + Br_2(l)

7. Ionic equation: NH_4^+(aq) + PO_4^{3-}(aq) + Ba^{2+}(aq) + OH^-(aq) → NH_4^+(aq) + OH^-(aq) + $Ba_3(PO_4)_2$(s); net ionic equation: PO_4^{3-}(aq) + Ba^{2+}(aq) → $Ba_3(PO_4)_2$(s); balanced net ionic equation: $2PO_4^{3-}$(aq) + $3Ba^{2+}$(aq) → $Ba_3(PO_4)_2$(s)

8. Ionic equation: Cu(s) + Ag^+(aq) + NO_3^-(aq) → Cu^{2+}(aq) + NO_3^-(aq) + Ag(s); net ionic equation: Cu(s) + Ag^+(aq) → Cu^{2+}(aq) + Ag(s); balanced net ionic equation: Cu(s) + $2Ag^+$(aq) → Cu^{2+}(aq) + $2Ag$(s) (Note: the charges have to balance too)

9. Ionic equation: Ca^{2+}(aq) + OH^-(aq) + H^+(aq) + SO_4^{2-}(aq) → $CaSO_4$(s) + H_2O(l); net ionic equation: Ca^{2+}(aq) + OH^-(aq) + H^+(aq) + SO_4^{2-}(aq) → $CaSO_4$(s) + H_2O(l); balanced net ionic equation: Ca^{2+}(aq) + OH^-(aq) + H^+(aq) + SO_4^{2-}(aq) → $CaSO_4$(s) + H_2O(l)

6·9

1. DD   2. S   3. D   4. C   5. SD

6·10   1. Products: $CdCl_2(aq)$ and $H_2(g)$; balanced equation: $Cd(s) + 2HCl(aq) \rightarrow CdCl_2(aq) + H_2(g)$

2. Products: $CO_2(g) + H_2O(g)$; balanced equation: $C_5H_{12}(g) + 8O_2(g) \rightarrow 5CO_2(g) + 6H_2O(g)$

3. Products: $NH_3(g)$; balanced equation: $N_2(g) + 3H_2(g) \rightarrow 2NH_3(g)$

4. Products: $BaSO_4(s) + AlCl_3(aq)$; balanced equation: $3BaCl_2(aq) + Al_2(SO_4)_3(aq) \rightarrow 3BaSO_4(s) + 2AlCl_3(aq)$

5. Products: $CuO(s) + H_2O(l)$; balanced equation: $Cu(OH)_2(s) \rightarrow CuO(s) + H_2O(l)$

7   Mass and mole relationships

7·1   1. Formula mass, 40.31 amu   2. Molecular mass, 108.02 amu   3. Formula mass, 78.08 amu
4. Molecular mass, 153.81 amu   5. Formula mass, 121.95 amu   6. Formula mass, 275.81 amu
7. Formula mass, 658.06 amu   8. Formula mass, 216.60 amu   9. Molecular mass, 20.01 amu
10. Molecular mass, 17.03 amu   11. Molecular mass, 80.07 amu   12. Formula mass, 142.05 amu
13. Formula mass, 187.57 amu   14. Formula mass, 197.31 amu   15. Formula mass, 149.10 amu
16. Formula mass, 74.55 amu   17. Molecular mass, 98.09 amu   18. Molecular mass, 28.01 amu
19. Formula mass, 56.11 amu   20. Formula mass, 262.87 amu

7·2   1. 28.01 g/mol   2. 60.09 g/mol   3. 76.02 g/mol   4. 159.62 g/mol   5. 133.10 g/mol   6. 30.01 g/mol
7. 40.00 g/mol   8. 87.92 g/mol   9. 134.45 g/mol   10. 97.57 g/mol   11. 253.80 g/mol   12. 92.02 g/mol
13. 132.15 g/mol   14. 47.02 g/mol   15. 18.02 g/mol   16. 32.00 g/mol   17. 166.94 g/mol
18. 56.38 g/mol   19. 108.82 g/mol   20. $Ca(OH)_2 = 74.10$ g/mol

7·3   1. 42.88% C; 57.12% O   2. 46.75% Si; 53.25% O   3. 36.86% N; 63.14% O   4. 39.81% Cu; 20.09% S;
40.10% O   5. 31.58% N; 9.087% H; 23.29% P 36.06% O (sometimes because of rounding the total
percentage exceeds 100%)   6. 46.68% N; 53.32% O   7. 57.48% Na; 40.00% O; 2.52% H   8. 63.52% Fe;
36.48% S   9. 47.27 % Cu; 52.73% Cl   10. 65.13% Cu; 32.80% O; 2.07% H   11. 100% I   12. 30.45% N;
69.55% O   13. 21.20% N; 6.10% H; 24.27%S; 48.43% O   14. 2.14% H; 29.80% N; 68.06% O
15. 11.19% H; 88.81% O   16. 100% O   17. 64.63% Ag; 14.39% C; 1.81% H; 19.17% O   18. 43.12% Mg;
56.88% S   19. 25.94% N; 74.06% O   20. 64.09% Ca; 43.18% O; 2.72% H (sometimes because of rounding
the total percentage is slightly below 100%)

7·4   1. 185 g   2. 0.128 mol   3. 1.20×10^{24} particles   4. 328 g   5. 1.81×10^{24} atoms   6. 6.82×10^{23}
atoms   7. 0.499 mol   8. 664 g   9. 0.871 mol   10. 0.0745 g   11. 3.46×10^{22} formula units
12. 1.20×10^{24} atoms   13. 0.107 mol   14. 385 g   15. 3.30×10^{24} atoms   16. 1.54×10^{24} atoms
17. 1.01×10^{23} atoms   18. 2.06 mol   19. 0.742 mol   20. 1.123×10^{24} atoms

7·5   1. $\dfrac{1\ \text{mol N}_2}{2\ \text{mol NH}_3}, \dfrac{3\ \text{mol H}_2}{2\ \text{mol NH}_3}$, and their reciprocals

2. $\dfrac{1\ \text{mol CH}_4}{1\ \text{mol CO}_2}, \dfrac{2\ \text{mol O}_2}{1\ \text{mol CO}_2}, \dfrac{1\ \text{mol CH}_4}{2\ \text{mol H}_2\text{O}}, \dfrac{2\ \text{mol O}_2}{2\ \text{mol H}_2\text{O}}$, and their reciprocals

3. $\dfrac{1\ \text{mol Na}_2\text{CO}_3}{2\ \text{mol NaCl}}, \dfrac{2\ \text{mol HCl}}{2\ \text{mol NaCl}}, \dfrac{1\ \text{mol Na}_2\text{CO}_3}{1\ \text{mol H}_2\text{O}}, \dfrac{2\ \text{mol HCL}}{1\ \text{mol H}_2\text{O}}$;

$\dfrac{1\ \text{mol Na}_2\text{CO}_3}{1\ \text{mol CO}_2}, \dfrac{2\ \text{mol HCl}}{1\ \text{mol CO}_2}$, and their reciprocals

4. $\dfrac{2\ \text{mol Na}}{2\ \text{mol NaCl}}, \dfrac{1\ \text{mol Cl}_2}{2\ \text{mol NaCl}}$, and their reciprocals

5. $\dfrac{1\ \text{mol Cl}_2}{2\ \text{mol KCl}}, \dfrac{2\ \text{mol KBr}}{2\ \text{mol KCl}}, \dfrac{1\ \text{mol Cl}_2}{1\ \text{mol Br}_2}, \dfrac{2\ \text{mol KBr}}{2\ \text{mol Br}_2}$, and their reciprocals

7·6   1. 42 mol   2. 28 mol   3. 50. mol   4. 48 mol   5. 80. mol   6. 88 mol   7. 2.0 mol   8. 3.9 mol
9. 11.6 mol of Fe and 8.7 mol of O_2 10. 1.8 mol

7·7   1. 108 g   2. 735 g   3. 1.76 g   4. 142 g   5. 77.5 g   6. 0.345 mol   7. 2.68 g   8. 1.65 g
9. 3.56×10^{22} atoms   10. 11.3 g   11. 2.2×10^{24} molecules   12. 8.13 g   13. 266 g   14. 0.471 mol of
$Al(NO_3)_3$ and 0.706 mol of H_2 15. 1.50×10^{26} atoms

7·8   1. Zn is the limiting reagent and 5.21 g of $ZnCl_2$ is produced.   2. HCl is the limiting reagent and 18.7 g of $ZnCl_2$ is produced.   3. HCl is the limiting reagent and 15.2 g of $ZnCl_2$ is produced.   4. Zn is the limiting reagent and 2.72 g of $ZnCl_2$ is produced.   5. HCl is the limiting reagent and 157 g of $ZnCl_2$ is produced.   6. HCl is the limiting reagent and 63.6 g of $ZnCl_2$ is produced.   7. HCl is the limiting reagent and 3.87 g of $ZnCl_2$ is produced.   8. HCl is the limiting reagent and 23.0 g of $ZnCl_2$ is produced.   9. Zn is the limiting reagent and 25.95 g of $ZnCl_2$ is produced.   10. HCl is the limiting reagent and 53 g of $ZnCl_2$ is produced.

7·9   1. 77.5%   2. 28 g   3. 53.9% (23.2 g of $Ni(OH)_2$ is the theoretical yield)   4. 94.3% (N_2 is the limiting reagent, producing 48.7 g of NH_3)   5. 79.1%   6. 46.0% (N_2 is the limiting reagent, producing 99.7 g of NH_3)   7. 854 %   8. 79%   9. 65%   10. 4.1%

7·10   1. *Formula mass* is the term used when the atoms are held together by an ionic bond, and *molecular mass* is the term used for a molecule held together by covalent bonds.   2. Molar mass is the mass of one mole of particles, measured in grams; formula and molecular mass are the mass in atomic mass units of one unit of a substance.   3. (a) 110.98 amu; (b) 234.80 amu; (c) 159.70 amu   4. (a) 20.01 amu; (b) 394.71 amu; (c) 283.88 amu   5. (a) 439.92 g/mol; (b) 108.02 g/mol; (c) 158.04 g/mol   6. (a) 1030 g; (b) 0.459 mol; (c) 2.76×10^{23} formula units; (d) 5.52×10^4 g   7. 3.07 g   8. (a) Nitrogen gas; (b) 6.38 g; (c) 6.39 g of hydrogen   9. 56.4%   10. 92.2%

8   Gas laws

8·1   1. 2.7 L   2. 1.84 atm   3. 23.8 L   4. 9.0 atm   5. 140 cm^3 6. The pressure is cut in half.   7. The volume is cut in half.   8. 0.80 L   9. 67 L   10. 1.1 atm

8·2   *If you are having difficulties with this section, remember that in all gas-law problems, the temperatures should be expressed in kelvins when setting up and solving the problem.* 1. 1.1 L   2. 48.3 L   3. 440 K or 170°C   4. 101 K or −172°C   5. 1.9 L   6. 1.4 L   7. 215 K or −58°C   8. 180 K or −97°C   9. 37.1 L   10. 6.3 L (When the temperature triples, the volume triples.)

8·3   1. 3.1 atm   2. 520 K or 250°C   3. 390 K or 120°C   4. 1,000 torr   5. 150 K or −130°C   6. 0.50 atm   7. 1.8 atm   8. 200 torr (Remember sig figs.)   9. 450 K or 170°C   10. 3.0 atm

8·4   1. 0.190 mol   2. 17 L   3. 8.07×10^{22} atoms   4. 6.02×10^{23} atoms, assuming the gas is monatomic   5. 0.835 mol   6. 4.5 mol   7. 3.01×10^{23} molecules   8. 30.7 L   9. 38.8 g   10. 0.156 mol

8·5

	P_1	V_1	T_1	P_2	V_2	T_2
1.	2.00 atm	1.25 L	100°C	1.00 atm	1.83 L	0.0°C
2.	55.5 mL	5.60 atm	20.0°C	3.50 atm	101 mL	60.0°C
3.	970 torr	2.1 L	−83°C	760 torr	4.2 L	25.0°C
4.	1,020 torr	250 mL	45.0°C	708 torr	326 mL	15.0°C
5.	1.00 atm	16 L	273 K	2.0 atm	12.0 L	400 K
6.	1,400 torr	2.80 L	25.5°C	750 torr	5.70 L	51.0°C
7.	0.98 atm	18.0 L	250 K	13 atm	1.65 L	301 K
8.	2.00 atm	1.25 L	200°C	1.500 atm	1.14 L	50.0°C
9.	1.00 atm	18.25 L	100°C	1.00 atm	12.5 L	−18.0°C
10.	760 torr	83 mL	250 K	0.88 atm	188 mL	500.0 K

8·6   1. 1.25 g/L   2. 2.86 g/L   3. 1.25 g/L   4. 2.05 g/L   5. 4.82 g/L

8·7   1. 71 g/mol   2. 3.12 g/L   3. 77.5 g/mol   4. 1.37 g/L   5. 140 g/mol

8·8   1. 56 L   2. 63 L   3. 121 g   4. 20.6 L   5. 1.50×10^2 g

8·9   1. $\dfrac{V_1}{T_1} = \dfrac{V_2}{T_2}$ 2. $P_1V_1 = P_2V_2$ 3. $\dfrac{P_1V_1}{T_1} = \dfrac{P_2V_2}{T_2}$ 4. $\dfrac{P_1}{T_1} = \dfrac{P_2}{T_2}$ 5. Avogadro's hypothesis

8·10   1. 1.86 L   2. 290 mL   3. 1.02 L   4. 1.26 atm   5. 75.4 L

9 Solutions

9·1 1. The powdered drink mix or the sugar and lemon juice are the solutes and the water is the solvent.
2. 3.672 M   3. 130 g   4. The coffee is the solvent.   5. 4.11 M   6. 14 g   7. 3.00 moles $C_6H_{12}O_6$
8. 30.0 moles   9. 1.46 g   10. 3.161 M

9·2 1. 0.88 M   2. 0.042 L   3. 3 M   4. 21 mL   5. 200 mL or 0.2 L   6. 0.45 M   7. 250 mL
8. 3.0 M   9. 67 g   10. You need to use all of the 0.500 M stock solution, because that provides you with the 0.025 mol of solute that you need for the 250 mL of 0.100 M solution. The 75 mL of 0.250 M solution will provide only 0.019 mol of solute, which is not enough to make the correct amount and concentration of solution that you need.

9·3 1. 8.0 *m*   2. 0.0250 mol   3. 4.0 kg   4. 3.8 *m*   5. 0.38 mol   6. 1.20 kg   7. 0.7173 *m*   8. 163 g
9. 1.84 kg   10. Neither, they contain the same number of moles of solute.

9·4 1. −3.7°C   2. 100.13°C   3. 24 mol   4. 6.7 mol   5. 10.0 mol   6. 1.3 mol   7. −2.7°C
8. 101.13°C   9. 48 g   10. 63 g

9·5 1. Na_2SO_4 2. NaCl   3. NH_3 4. $NaNO_3$ 5. KNO_3 6. About 43°C   7. Approximately 68 g
8. Approximately 135 g   9. Approximately 42 g   10. Approximately 72 g   11. Saturated
12. Unsaturated   13. Supersaturated   14. Approximately 17 g

9·6 1. 1.3 M   2. 0.329 M   3. 0.445 M   4. 3.35 M   5. 640 g   6. 30 g   7. 1.18 M   8. 5.0×10^2 mL
9. 10. *m*   10. 2.00 *m*   11. 3.2 *m*   12. 1.5 mol   13. 2,010 g   14. −4.89°C   15. 101.37°C

10 Acids and bases

10·1 1. Pair 1: $H_3O^+(aq)$ and $H_2O(l)$; pair 2: $HNO_3(aq)$ and $NO_3^-(aq)$
2. Pair 1: $H_2O(l)$ and $OH^-(aq)$; pair 2: $HSO_4^-(aq)$ and $SO_4^{2-}(aq)$
3. Pair 1: $H_2O(l)$ and $OH^-(aq)$; pair 2: $H_2SO_4(aq)$ and $HSO_4^-(aq)$
4. Pair 1: $H_3O^+(aq)$ and $H_2O(l)$; pair 2: $HC_2H_3O_2(aq)$ and $C_2H_3O_2^-(aq)$
5. Pair 1: $H_2S(g)$ and $HS^-(aq)$; pair 2: $H_3O^+(aq)$ and $H_2O(l)$
6. Pair 1: $H_2PO_4^-(aq)$ and $HPO_4^{2-}(aq)$; pair 2: $H_2O(l)$ and $OH^-(aq)$
7. Pair 1: $H_3O^+(aq)$ and $H_2O(l)$; pair 2: $HClO_3(aq)$ and $ClO_3^-(aq)$
8. Pair 1: $HBrO(aq)$ and $BrO^-(aq)$; pair 2: $H_3O^+(aq)$ and $H_2O(l)$
9. Pair 1: $HCl(aq)$ and $Cl^-(aq)$; pair 2: $NH_4^+(aq)$ and $NH_3(aq)$
10. Pair 1: $H_3O^+(aq)$ and $H_2O(l)$; pair 2: $HX(aq)$ and $X^-(aq)$

10·2 1. Acidic   2. Basic   3. Acidic   4. Acidic   5. Neutral   6. Acidic   7. Basic   8. Basic
9. Acidic   10. Basic

10·3 1. Red   2. Blue   3. Red   4. Red   5. Red   6. Red   7. Blue   8. Blue   9. Red   10. Blue

10·4 1. Red   2. Blue   3. Red   4. Red   5. Blue   6. Red   7. Blue   8. Blue   9. Red   10. Blue

10·5 1. (a) base; (b) acid; (c) neutral; (d) base; (e) acid; (f) base; (g) base; (h) acid; (i) acid; (j) base
2. (a) weak; (b) strong; (c) strong; (d) weak; (e) weak; (f) weak; (g) weak; (h) weak; (i) strong; (j) weak

10·6 1. 2.00   2. 0.60   3. 0.30   4. −0.60   5. −0.78   6. 4.0×10^{-7} M   7. 2×10^{-12} M   8. 3.2×10^{-2} M
9. 6×10^{-4} M   10. 8×10^{-10} M   11. 4.74   12. 1.51   13. 1.89

10·7 1. Weak   2. Strong   3. Strong   4. Weak   5. Weak   6. Weak   7. Strong   8. Weak
9. Strong   10. Weak

10·8 1. 11.0   2. 6.5   3. The substance in question 1 is acidic and the substance in question 2 is slightly basic.
4. 1.00   5. 13.00   6. −0.78   7. 14.78   8. 1.0×10^{-6} M   9. 11.88   10. 12.04

10·9 1. 11.2   2. pH = 2.07, pOH = 11.93   3. 2×10^{-7} M   4. 10.5   5. $[H^+] = 5.6 \times 10^{-10}$ M, $[OH^-] = 1.8 \times 10^{-5}$ M   6. $[H^+] = 2.8 \times 10^{-3}$ M, $[OH^-] = 3.5 \times 10^{-12}$ M   7. 3.5   8. pH = 13.88, pOH = 0.12
9. 2×10^{-5} M   10. 1×10^{-8} M

10·10 1. Pair 1: H_3O^+(aq) and H_2O(l); pair 2: HBr(aq) and Br^-(aq)
2. Pair 1: H_2O(l) and OH^-(aq); pair 2: CH_3COOH(aq) and CH_3COO^-(aq)
3. Pair 1: H_2SO_4(aq) and HSO_4^-(aq); pair 2: H_3O^+(aq) and H_2O
4. Pair 1: H_3PO_4(aq) and $H_2PO_4^-$(aq); pair 2: H_3O^+(aq) and H_2O(l)
5. Pair 1: $H_2PO_4^-$(aq) and HPO_4^{2-}(aq); pair 2: H_3O^+(aq) and H_2O(l)

10·11 1. Basic   2. Acidic   3. Acidic   4. Basic   5. Acidic   6. Acidic   7. Basic   8. Basic
9. Neutral   10. Acidic

10·12 1. Blue; blue   2. Red; red   3. Red; red   4. Blue; blue   5. Red; red   6. Red; red
7. Blue; blue   8. Blue; blue   9. Red; blue   10. Red; red

10·13 1. Acid, strong   2. Base, strong   3. Base, weak   4. Acid, weak   5. Acid, weak   6. Acid, strong
7. Base, strong   8. Base, weak   9. Base, weak   10. Acid, weak

10·14 1. pOH = 5.85, $[H^+] = 7.1 \times 10^{-9}$ M, and $[OH^-] = 1.4 \times 10^{-6}$ M   2. pH = 0.4, $[H^+] = 4 \times 10^{-1}$ M, and $[OH^-] = 3 \times 10^{-14}$ M   3. pH = 10.635, pOH = 3.365, and $[H^+] = 2.32 \times 10^{-11}$ M   4. pH = 5.10, pOH = 8.90, and $[OH^-] = 1.3 \times 10^{-9}$ M   5. pH = 7.000, pOH = 7.000, and $[H^+] = 1.00 \times 10^{-7}$ M

11 Thermochemistry

11·1 1. 50.7 cal   2. 3100 J   3. 0.22 kJ   4. 84,000 cal   5. 4.14 kJ   6. 53,800 cal   7. 405,000 J
8. 0.0350 kcal   9. 836 J   10. 36,000 cal

11·2 1. 113 °C   2. 1920 J   3. 23,500 J or 23.5 kJ   4. 185 J   5. 1.80×10^3 J or 1.80 kJ   6. 6°C
7. 44.9°C   8. 115,000 J or 115 kJ   9. 90,000 J or 490 kJ   10. 0.62 J/g°C

11·3 1. 1.74 J/g°C   2. 0.45 J/g°C   3. 5.20 J/g°C   4. 2.26 J/g°C   5. 2.06 J/g°C   6. 45.8 J/°C   7. 2,300 J/°C   8. 550. J/°C   9. 941,000 J/°C   10. 295 J/°C

11·4 1. 9.0°C   2. 133,000 J   3. 6.49°C   4. 93.2°C   5. 58.9°C

11·5 1. 18.3°C   2. 15.6°C   3. 171 g   4. $c = 0.750$ J/g°C. The compound is SiO_2.   5. 27°C   6. 13.5°C
7. $c = 0.525$ J/g°C. The metal is Ti.   8. 9.19°C   9. 105 g   10. 29.7°C

11·6 1. 25 J   2. 6.0×10^3 J or 6.0 kJ   3. 510 J   4. 1,116 J   5. 1,720 J

11·7 1. 15,000 or 1.5×10^4 J   2. 138 cal   3. 239 cal   4. 960,000 J or 9.6×10^5 J   5. 842 cal   6. $m = q/c\Delta T$
7. $c = q/m\Delta T$ 8. $\Delta T = q/mc$ 9. $T_f = (q/mc) + T_i$ 10. $T_i = T_f - (q/mc)$ 11. $m = C/c$ 12. $c = C/m$
13. $T_f = (m_1c_1T_1 + m_2c_2T_2)/(m_1c_1 + m_2c_2)$ 14. $m_1 = (m_2c_2\Delta T_2)/(c_1\Delta T_1)$ 15. $c_1 = (m_2c_2\Delta T_2)/(m_1\Delta T_1)$;
the identity of substance 1 is found by looking on a table of specific heats.

Periodic Table of the Elements

Atomic number

| 10 |
| **Ne** |
| Neon |
| 20.18 |

Approximate average atomic mass.

1 1A	2 2A		3 3B	4 4B	5 5B	6 6B	7 7B	8	9 8B	10	11 1B	12 2B	13 3A	14 4A	15 5A	16 6A	17 7A	18 8A
1 **H** Hydrogen 1.008																		2 **He** Helium 4.003
3 **Li** Lithium 6.941	4 **Be** Beryllium 9.012												5 **B** Boron 10.81	6 **C** Carbon 12.01	7 **N** Nitrogen 14.01	8 **O** Oxygen 16.00	9 **F** Fluorine 19.00	10 **Ne** Neon 20.18
11 **Na** Sodium 22.99	12 **Mg** Magnesium 24.31												13 **Al** Aluminum 26.98	14 **Si** Silicon 28.09	15 **P** Phosphorus 30.97	16 **S** Sulfur 32.07	17 **Cl** Chlorine 35.45	18 **Ar** Argon 39.95
19 **K** Potassium 39.10	20 **Ca** Calcium 40.08		21 **Sc** Scandium 44.96	22 **Ti** Titanium 47.88	23 **V** Vanadium 50.94	24 **Cr** Chromium 52.00	25 **Mn** Manganese 54.94	26 **Fe** Iron 55.85	27 **Co** Cobalt 58.93	28 **Ni** Nickel 58.69	29 **Cu** Copper 63.55	30 **Zn** Zinc 65.39	31 **Ga** Gallium 69.72	32 **Ge** Germanium 72.59	33 **As** Arsenic 74.92	34 **Se** Selenium 78.96	35 **Br** Bromine 79.90	36 **Kr** Krypton 83.80
37 **Rb** Rubidium 85.47	38 **Sr** Strontium 87.62		39 **Y** Yttrium 88.91	40 **Zr** Zirconium 91.22	41 **Nb** Niobium 92.91	42 **Mo** Molybdenum 95.94	43 **Tc** Technetium (98)	44 **Ru** Ruthenium 101.1	45 **Rh** Rhodium 102.9	46 **Pd** Palladium 106.4	47 **Ag** Silver 107.9	48 **Cd** Cadmium 112.4	49 **In** Indium 114.8	50 **Sn** Tin 118.7	51 **Sb** Antimony 121.8	52 **Te** Tellurium 127.6	53 **I** Iodine 126.9	54 **Xe** Xenon 131.3
55 **Cs** Cesium 132.9	56 **Ba** Barium 137.3		57 **La** Lanthanum 138.9	72 **Hf** Hafnium 178.5	73 **Ta** Tantalum 180.9	74 **W** Tungsten 183.9	75 **Re** Rhenium 186.2	76 **Os** Osmium 190.2	77 **Ir** Iridium 192.2	78 **Pt** Platinum 195.1	79 **Au** Gold 197.0	80 **Hg** Mercury 200.6	81 **Tl** Thallium 204.4	82 **Pb** Lead 207.2	83 **Bi** Bismuth 209.0	84 **Po** Polonium (210)	85 **At** Astatine (210)	86 **Rn** Radon (222)
87 **Fr** Francium (223)	88 **Ra** Radium (226)		89 **Ac** Actinium (227)	104 **Rf** Rutherfordium (257)	105 **Db** Dubnium (260)	106 **Sg** Seaborgium (263)	107 **Bh** Bohrium (262)	108 **Hs** Hassium (265)	109 **Mt** Meitnerium (266)	110 **Ds** Darmstadtium (269)	111 **Rg** Roentgenium (272)	112	113	114	115	116	(117)	118

58 **Ce** Cerium 140.1	59 **Pr** Praseodymium 140.9	60 **Nd** Neodymium 144.2	61 **Pm** Promethium (147)	62 **Sm** Samarium 150.4	63 **Eu** Europium 152.0	64 **Gd** Gadolinium 157.3	65 **Tb** Terbium 158.9	66 **Dy** Dysprosium 162.5	67 **Ho** Holmium 164.9	68 **Er** Erbium 167.3	69 **Tm** Thulium 168.9	70 **Yb** Ytterbium 173.0	71 **Lu** Lutetium 175.0
90 **Th** Thorium 232.0	91 **Pa** Protactinium (231)	92 **U** Uranium 238.0	93 **Np** Neptunium (237)	94 **Pu** Plutonium (242)	95 **Am** Americium (243)	96 **Cm** Curium (247)	97 **Bk** Berkelium (247)	98 **Cf** Californium (249)	99 **Es** Einsteinium (254)	100 **Fm** Fermium (253)	101 **Md** Mendelevium (256)	102 **No** Nobelium (254)	103 **Lr** Lawrencium (257)

Metals

Metalloids

Nonmetals